THE 7 FIGURE SUMMER

How To Build A Door-To-Door Sales Empire

by

Adam Webb

Contents

Introduction

It's Saturday morning. My alarm clock is screaming at me to get out of bed. I look at the time. I need to get up, eat, dress, and be at the morning meeting in ten minutes. I tell myself I can do those things in less than five minutes and hit the snooze. Or at least I thought I hit the snooze. Maybe I just hit off. Either way, the next thing to wake me up is my phone buzzing incessantly. I see it's my sales manager. I also see the time and realize that I missed the meeting. I silence the call and notice the barrage of texts he had sent during my slumber. "Don't be late!", "Meeting is starting!", "Where are you??", "I'm outside your apartment! Hurry up, we are leaving!!" I roll out of bed, throw on the closest knocking shirt I could find on the ground, grab a couple of things and head out the door. I hop in the front seat of my sales manager call, let him know I'm ready for the day, recline the seat, and fall back asleep.

After what seemed like a short rest, we arrived at my knocking area. I stepped out of the car and waved goodbye. It's a warm and sunny San Diego summer morning. I pretended to look at my knocking notes as my manager drove off. I watched his car out of the corner of my eye. As soon as he turned out of site. I pulled out my phone and eagerly texted my exact location to a buddy.

After a short while, he pulls up. I excitedly jump into his car, and together we head for the beach. We grab breakfast burritos at Albertos before heading to 11th street in Del Mar to enjoy an epic afternoon of surfing. About twenty minutes before sunset, my buddy drops me off at the exact spot where he picked me up. Shortly after, I see my sales manager round the corner down the street and approach. Before he gets close enough to see me, I blow as much salt water as I can out of each nostril. I hop in his car and he asks me how knocking went. I inform him I unfortunately hadn't sold anything all day!

I began my career in door-to-door sales with about as low ambition and low expectations as anyone could. Nothing in my life up to that point had led me to believe that I could accomplish anything beyond mediocrity. Aside from two years of charitable service, the previous decade of my life had been characterized by nothing more than satisfying my own desire for nonstop fun and laziness! And so when I signed up to do door-to-door sales, I behaved in harmony with my lack luster vision, which included substituting knocking with surfing and sleeping whenever I possibly could! This wouldn't last forever, though.

About a year later, my vision for myself was elevated when a leader I respected called me out of the blue one day. This leader informed me he had been observing me and felt I had the potential to perform at a high level. He believed that I could rank among the top sales reps in my company and earn $100,000 that summer. I don't know if it was because I looked up to him or because I desperately needed a change in my life, but whatever the reason, when he shared his vision for me, I believed him. This conversation changed how I viewed myself. I saw myself as someone that could dominate the doors like all the top sales reps I admired. Once my vision changed, my behavior changed.

I began studying daily, working harder, knocking more doors, and seeking the training, tools, mentorship, and coaching I needed to make this new vision a reality. I became the number one sales rep in my company that year, achieved my first six-figure summer, and leveled up in a way I didn't think was possible. I became a consistent top performer on the doors. The personal growth I experienced felt incredible. But it didn't last.

Eventually, I hit my sales cap. There were only so many hours in a day for me to make sales and I was consistently maximizing them all. I was making incredible money, winning competitions, and receiving all the recognition I could ever hope for, but I wasn't growing. I had hit a plateau and now felt stagnant. I saw no potential for myself beyond "top sales rep." The thought of growing into the role of sales manager and running a sales team had never even crossed my mind.

For six years, I continued to sell until a change of circumstance forced me to expand my vision again. The sales team I was on had grown large, and a new market had opened up that needed a manager. My company asked me to step in and manage that team. I chatted with the owner of my company, and he told me he believed I would be an effective and successful sales manager. I don't know if it was because I looked up to him or because I desperately needed more growth in my life, but whatever the reason, when he shared his vision for me, I believed him.

This conversation changed how I viewed myself. I saw myself as someone that could dominate sales management like all the top sales leaders. Once my vision changed, my behavior changed. I began studying books on leadership, recruiting, systems, management, influence, and human behavior. I spent time off the doors thinking about the culture and experience I wanted reps to experience in my sales program.

I crushed it my first year managing. I doubled my income. I positively affected other people's lives, and I loved it. I continued to grow in my role as sales manager for several years, each year achieving new heights.

But it didn't last.

Eventually, I hit my cap. There were only so many people I could manage effectively. My team got so large that the growth tapered off. I was making life-changing money, my team was winning competitions, and we were getting recognition on stage at company events, but we weren't growing. I had hit a plateau and felt stagnant again. I saw no potential for myself beyond "top sales manager". The thought of regionally managing multiple sales teams had never even crossed my mind. For five years, I managed until a change of circumstances forced me to expand my vision once again.

Within my massive team, I had two leaders who hated each other. They couldn't be in the same room. At company events, they butted heads, made undercutting comments to each other in meetings, and each constantly complained in private about the other. It was looking like it would be rough summer. I didn't know what to do. So I consulted a sales leader in my company I respected. He told me it was time to split my team and empower my two leaders to each manage half as separate offices. I was confused and wondered where that left me. He explained I would become a regional manager and oversee both the offices. He told me he believed I would be an effective and successful leader of leaders. He told me I was an incredible coach, mentor, and leader and would thrive in the role as regional manager. I don't know if it was because I looked up to him or because I desperately needed to grow, but whatever the reason, when he shared his vision for me, I believed him. This conversation changed how I viewed myself. I saw myself as someone that could grow a massive sales program. The top sales program in the industry. Like the titans of my industry I admired. Once my vision changed, my behavior changed.

I studied books on business, marketing, culture, and finance. I built systems that would create great leaders instead of just great sales reps. And I became one of the fastest growing regionals in my company. I embraced my new role fully, developed incredible leaders, oversaw multiple teams, grew my income and my organization, and loved every second of it.

I look back on my journey in door-to-door sales with profound gratitude. The doors made me who I am, gave me incredible income and, more importantly, incredible experiences. But I also look back and realize that what took fourteen years to accomplish could've been done in just four.

My career in door-to-door was an incredible but also very long process of slowly expanding my vision and gradually gathering the tools I needed to level up from sales to management to eventually becoming a leader of leaders. Along my journey, I was blessed to know, work with, and be mentored by the best sales recruiters and leaders in door-to-door, including top performers from multiple different companies and industries. Throughout my career, I kept meticulous notes on these conversations, my personal experiences, insights, and epiphanies related to sales recruiting, leadership, and organizational growth.

It is said that a smart man learns from his mistakes, but a wise man learns from the mistakes of others.

I wrote The Seven-Figure Summer so that everyone in door-to-door sales can learn from my experiences and achieve what I achieved faster. This book will expand your vision and give you the tools you need to recruit a massive door-to-door sales organization, develop into a world-class sales leader, and avoid countless pitfalls and mistakes that I experienced throughout my years on the doors. The Seven-Figure Summer outlines the exact principles, practices, and process that have catapulted so many to seven-figure recruiting incomes. It's a book written for door-to-door sales leaders, by a door-to-door sales leader. It represents the most potent document ever assembled on the subject of sales recruiting!

Why should you read The Seven-Figure Summer?

To you, the reader, I ask, what will be your lasting impact in life? How much of your contribution to the world will remain when you're gone, and how long will it remain? Eventually, every door you ever knocked, every product you ever pitched, and every person you ever sold will all be dust. Think about that for a second. Literally every door you knocked on recently will eventually be buried in a landfill, along with every roof, alarm, smart home system, solar array, and everything else. Eventually, your customers, and you will all be gone. So, what will remain of all your work?

In the end, your influence is the only thing that can last forever. Your lasting impact perpetuates in the people whose thoughts, feelings, and behaviors you affected for the better and continues through as they, in turn, positively affect others. There is no nobler ambition than to positively influence other people.

As stated by the Rastafarian musician Bob Marley, "The greatness of a man is not in how much wealth he acquires, but in his integrity and his ability to affect those around him positively."

Your influence not only determines your lasting impact but also determines your income! The amount of money you will make this year is directly proportionate to the amount of people you influence and how deeply you influence them (see Chapter Six: Measuring Leadership). This book will teach you how to attract staggering amounts of people to you so that you can positively affect their lives and leave a permanent source of value of this Earth, all while making life-changing money in the process. You should read this book because it will not only help you turn recruiting into a multi-million dollar opportunity but will allow you to change lives and leave a legacy.

Before you begin, however, please recognize that the information that follows is absolutely useless if you have not made an internal commitment to live what you learn. Specifically, you must agree to the following:

1.   You are willing to discard preconceived notions you may hold about recruiting.

2.   You are willing to attack your fears by voluntarily placing yourself far outside of your comfort zone.

3.   You are willing to raise your work ethic to new and uncomfortable levels.

If you are willing to take this challenge in the hope of exponentially increasing your influence and income, then let's begin.

Note that most of the quotes in this book came from interviews that the author conducted with recruiters who had each made over one million dollars in one year through recruiting. These quotes are italicized and blocked into large single paragraphs. A new paragraph always means a quote from a new source.

Chapter 1
Why Recruit?
It's not what you think!

Hopefully, your heart and mind are burning with desire to learn how to recruit! But before tackling the question of "How?", there's a more important question to answer first: "Why?" Why should you recruit? Especially if you are already making great money selling door-to-door, why spend the extra time and energy recruiting, training, and managing other sales reps?

Money is an awesome byproduct of recruiting, but the reality is that earning seven figures through recruiting poses such difficulty, that money alone will not be a sufficient enough motivator to get you there. You need to understand the deeper purpose that drives the process. As Jim Rohn so simply stated, "the bigger the why, the easier the how." Fully understanding why you should make the commitment to recruit will give you the power to actually see the process through. There are three compelling reasons for recruiting, that if correctly understood, should create a large enough "why" to make the "hows" of recruiting easily attainable.

Why Recruit? Reason Number One
When It Comes To Door-to-Door, You Recruit, Or You Die

Door-to-door sales is the greatest income opportunity of all time. It's like a money faucet. You drive to a neighborhood, knock on doors, and get paid more than doctors, lawyers, and CEOs. So what is the problem? Why can't you just keep selling forever? Why do you need to recruit and grow? As you learned from my personal story, it's because personal production always has a cap, and when you hit that ceiling, you will begin to die professionally. Sales without recruiting is a ticking time bomb.

"Never forget this. The individuals who only focus on their personal sales eventually die. I've noticed over

*the years that it's hard to get recruits back if they
don't make more than they did the year before. It
doesn't matter if you make ten-thousand or two-
hundred-thousand dollars. If your income is not
increasing, you're just going to be disappointed.
Professional satisfaction goes far beyond the money.
It's the feeling of accomplishment that keeps people
around. That said, there's only two ways you can
make more money in sales: sell more, or recruit. The
problem with selling is there's a cap. You can only
reach a certain limit. You max out your potential in
earning and accomplishment, and when that happens
it's game over. But there is no cap in recruiting. The
possibility for growth and earning is literally
unlimited."*

In other words, professional satisfaction and stoke
doesn't come from money, it comes from progress.
It's not about the dollars, it's about the growth. But
sustainable growth is impossible if it is only based on
your personal production. The imperative, therefore,
is to recruit.

*"There's only so many hours in the day. There's only
so many doors I can knock. So as good of a salesman*

as I was, I knew that selling alone would never get me to where I wanted to be. You can't sell indefinitely, there's a cap. Even if you are the top sales rep year after year, there's still a cap. But recruiting is endless. A sale is only ever going to be worth some fixed amount. But if you recruit one individual it literally could be worth a million dollars to you. Think of selling and recruiting as throwing a rock in a pond. Your personal sales is just the splash. Recruiting is the ripple that goes on forever."

If you want to continue to derive meaning and satisfaction from your career in door-to-door, you have to recruit. There's no other choice. If you don't recruit, you are working toward your eventual door-to-door demise. Don't let the fact that you may have several good years of personal sales growth ahead deter you from recruiting right now. This is a huge mistake that many in door-to-door fall prey to. Eventually, you will maximize your sales potential and your upward trajectory will halt.

Do not allow yourself to smack into the death cap or be blindsided by the performance plateau. If you allow your growth to stagnate, you will find yourself stuck in a job that pays you great money but that you no longer love. Instead, begin now to position yourself for limitless accomplishment, limitless success, limitless satisfaction, and limitless earning!

Why Recruit? Reason Number Two
You Are Already a Master of It

Growing up in San Diego, I developed a profound love for the ocean and became an avid surfer at a young age. Surfing requires a lot of practice— it requires balance in all directions and you must develop reflexes in every part of your body, even your toes! But while surfing seems like an extremely difficult sport, it's ultimately just muscle memory. In time, my body learned exactly how to position itself and how much weight and pressure to distribute on the board to be able to ride awesome waves. Once I learned these fundamentals, surfing was an absolute blast.

Moving to Utah, there were no waves to ride, but there were mountains! I decided snowboarding would become a satisfactory substitute for surfing.

Snowboarding, like surfing, is tricky to learn. It requires muscle memory and reflexes in every part of your body. If it took years to learn to surf, how long would it take me to learn how to snowboard? I was happy to discover that, unlike surfing, I was able to learn snowboarding in virtually no time! Why was I able to master snowboarding so quickly?

The principles of weight distribution and balance in snowboarding are nearly identical to surfing. I learned to look at a mountain slope as just another giant wave. I took what I had learned in the water and applied it to the snow. All that was required to transfer my mastery was a solid and consistent effort and a willingness to take some good falls. Before long, I was up and ripping the snow!

Surfing is to snowboarding what sales is to recruiting. Mastery in one is mastery in the other. As a sales rep, the time and energy you have spent building your skill in sales is time and energy that you have simultaneously spent perfecting the craft of recruiting; development in one is development in the other. All you need is to be willing to make a solid and consistent effort at recruiting and be willing to wipe-out every now and again. If you're ok investing

WHY RECRUIT?

Because you're already great at it.

a little effort in transferring your skill to a new craft, you'll be up and ripping in no time too! As one recruiter put it,

"I always treat recruiting like the sales process. Don't differentiate the two skills, they're the same thing. Just apply the steps of selling to recruiting: Prospect, Present, and Close."

After interviewing multiple millionaire recruiters, it became unquestionably apparent—if you can sell, you can recruit. Period. Over and over again I heard this phrase repeated: "It's like selling." As you study this program, notice how frequently the best lessons in recruiting are drawn from experiences selling door-to-door. In fact, if you look back at the table of contents, you'll see that the recruiting process outlined is just the sales cycle: prospect, qualify, present, overcoming objections, and close!

Before transitioning to "Why Recruit? Reason #3" I want to address a common concern about recruiting. Many people, including very successful sales reps, have tried recruiting in the past and failed. Maybe that was you. Does this mean you're destined to forever remain a sales rep? No way. Don't fret, there's more people in your shoes than you think. I asked a bunch of successful recruiters the following question: "What would you say to someone who tried recruiting in the past, didn't see success, and gave up on it?"

They gave three main reasons why aspiring recruiters fail. As you read their responses, be honest with yourself and contemplate if some of their statements might apply to you. If even only one does, decide right now to give recruiting another chance.

Failure Reason #1: You didn't stick with it long enough.

"A mistake recruiters make is that they try recruiting, fail a couple of times, it feels personal to them for some reason, so they give up. But it's just like sales; If you stop knocking after your tenth 'no', you're never going to find that person that's gonna give you a 'yes.' If you want to sell accounts and you're getting told no, what do you do? You go knock on more doors. The only person who can tell you it doesn't work is you. If anyone says they're no good at

recruiting, that just means they haven't done it long enough. People are afraid of recruiting only because they haven't learned how to do it. People don't fear what they know or have mastered. Recruiting only sucks when you don't know how to do it, and the only way to gain mastery is to work at it."

Here's another recruiter's perspective.

"Welcome to life. It takes time to become a good recruiter and figure out what process works for you exactly. Unless you consistently try, you're never going to figure it out. And that goes for anything, no matter what you're trying to accomplish in life. My first year managing I got my butt kicked. I could've quit and said, 'this isn't for me' and gone a different route, but I stuck it out. Consistency is the key!"

Failure Reason #2: You weren't fully committed.

"If you fail to commit then you commit to fail. Recruiting is not a one-time or one-year event, it's a process. You need to remember there are always hungry, ambitious people out there that need money.

There's always a fresh batch of them every single year."

Being committed involves being willing to pay the price. You must believe that if you commit, in time, you will succeed.

"It's harder than you think, but you can do it. I gave up on recruiting several times. If it wasn't for one individual encouraging me, I never would have progressed to becoming a sales manager. Most people don't believe that they can recruit a team, but the truth is everybody can recruit."

Failure Reason #3: Your desire was weak.

"One of the things with recruiting is you have to want it. I don't know a single person that's really tried recruiting that hasn't succeeded. Think of selling, what do you say to a rep that went out and tried to sell, didn't sell any accounts and quit? You probably tell him he didn't give it everything he's got, or he quit too soon. If somebody really wants to recruit they're going to go figure out ways to recruit. If they

don't truly want to recruit, then they're going to quit. They're going to fail a couple times and give up. The thing that I've learned is that the person that wants it the most usually wins."

In summary, if it didn't work the last time, it's probably because you didn't actually want it bad enough or you quit too soon. Be objective and assess if this might be the case. If it is, hit the reset button and begin plowing toward your seven-figure income —try again! Remember, if you can sell, you can recruit! Take confidence and commit! Let's jump back and discuss the final reason why you should recruit.

Why Recruit? Reason Number 3
It Will Completely Change Your Life

One question elicited a particularly powerful emotional response from every recruiter I interviewed.

"What has recruiting done for your life?"

Their answers made it abundantly clear that there is no professional activity that will have a more meaningful and positive impact on your life than recruiting. Here's a list of responses to this question. Remember that each new paragraph is a different response from a different recruiter.

"It's so much more than the money. People just don't understand what they can become through the process of recruiting. Recruiting is everything. It's provided my livelihood, great relationships, and a lot of practical know-how. It's provided deep personal satisfaction for me and thousands of other people. Recruiting is what's fed our company and our people. It's created everything I love around me."
"It's given my life purpose. I'm able to provide people with an absolutely amazing opportunity. The same opportunity I had—actually an even better opportunity."

"We need to broaden our vision of what the real opportunity is in recruiting. You can be a great salesperson, but ultimately if you want to succeed at the highest level and increase your income rapidly,

WHY RECRUIT?

Because it will absolutely change your life.

you have to put the time and effort into recruiting and learn how to enjoy the process. Be willing to build and recruit and don't be afraid to accept and internalize the vision."

"Why wouldn't you want to quadruple your income? And why wouldn't you want to help others have the same opportunities that you have had? I don't get it. I really don't understand why everyone doesn't recruit. I loved selling, and I'm good at it, but recruiting is different. Recruiting is something I can do as a career, and I never get tired of it. I genuinely enjoy it. I could do it all day and not even feel like I've worked."

"A lot of our people just don't understand what the recruiting opportunity is. Even our very best managers don't actually see the job for what it could really be. We miss big opportunities to create real value because we only see the small picture. Recruiting becomes as easy as breathing when you actually understand the opportunity."

"Recruiting has made me a multi-millionaire. I don't know how to say it any nicer or more humble than

that. It's given me the experience of growing a business and allowed me to earn passive income. As good as selling was and as much as I made, it doesn't even compare to what I've made recruiting. Your ability to take rejection and the pain that comes from recruiting is going to determine your income level. It really is. Besides, recruiting is fun! It's kept me happy and young. It's helped me become a better listener and problem solver. I love sitting down with a recruit, really listening and figuring out what is making them doubt themselves. Then just helping them totally eliminate that doubt, have confidence in themselves, and go have a great experience. For me, that's the best. That's everything right there."

What opportunity could be better than making over one million dollars in a single year and changing people's lives in the process? If you want to stay stoked on door-to-door, monetize a skill you've already developed (sales), and absolutely change your life, then start recruiting right now! You have nothing to lose!

Recruiting becomes as easy as breathing when you actually understand the **opportunity.**

Chapter 1
Why Recruit?
Summary & Action Items

- Recruiting is a choice, but it's a choice you should make for the following reasons:

- It's the only way to avoid peaking and collapsing in your door-to-door career.

- You are already incredible at it.

- It will absolutely change your life in ways you can't even imagine.

- If you failed before, it was likely for one of the following reasons. Commit to try again!

  You didn't stick with it long enough.
  You weren't fully committed.
  Your desire was weak.

Take a moment to consider what your life would look like if you truly maximized the recruiting opportunity. Journal answers to the following questions.

How would earning over a million dollars in a year change your life?

What type of person would you become through that process?

What type of positive impact would you have on other people?

Hopefully at this point you unequivocally understand why you must recruit. And with that big why firmly planted in your mind, we can now tackle the "how" of recruiting.

Chapter Two
PROSPECTING
Where do I find top talent?

After graduating high school, I signed up for two years of full-time service with my church. I was assigned to New England and after I finished, I returned home to San Diego. I was twenty-one years old with a one-point-something high school GPA and no resume, so I took the first job I was offered and got to work as a drug dealer (the legal kind). My buddy's dad owned a pharmacy in town, and part of his service included delivering medicine to customers that couldn't drive. So every day, I would load up a van full of prescriptions, and head out on a cross-county tour of San Diego to drop off the goods! Most of my high school friends were away at college, and I found myself pretty lonely and bored. My days were spent driving around during the day, watching animal planet reruns with my dad in the evening, and sleeping in the closet of his storage room at night. I didn't know what I wanted to do with my life, but I felt like I wasn't getting it in San Diego. So at the suggestion of an ex-girlfriend, I packed up and moved to Provo, Utah.

Besides her, I did not know a single person in the entire state. I didn't even know who my roommates were until the day I moved in. (One of them had 13 fingers!) Not knowing anybody made things difficult when I eventually decided that I wanted to be a professional recruiter.

I had watched as recruiters who grew up in Utah fished from seemingly endless pools of high school friends and hometown homies. Everyone seemed to know each other. I concluded that because I had no network in Utah, that recruiting was not going to work out for me. I just didn't have the resources that everyone else had. How could I recruit people if I don't know people?

As it turned out, my paradigm just needed to take a massive shift. Through a LOT of trial and error, I discovered that professional recruiting is not about who you know, it's about what you know. My lack of network was not the problem, my lack of training was. Once I learned how to recruit and started treating recruiting like a profession instead of a casual side job, I found myself outperforming the "well-connected" recruiters. Their vast networks actually acted like a crutch, preventing them from learning and mastering professional recruiting practices that I had no choice but to learn.

This chapter will teach you how to open up unlimited pools of prospects. You will have more recruits than you know what to do with! Instead of spending years figuring out how to prospect for recruits through trial-and-error, you will benefit from knowledge that came from decades of trial-and-error by myself and other professional recruiters.

Specifically, we will discuss sources, methods, and metrics of recruiting prospecting.

Prospecting Sources

All recruiting prospects can be categorized in two ways: cold contacts and warm contacts.

Cold recruits are people with whom you have no previous connection. They're strangers. You find cold recruits through social media and job postings, in-person shoulder tapping at malls or colleges, running recruiting booths, talking to people you run into as you go throughout your day (known as opening your mouth everywhere), etc.

Warm recruits are people with whom you have a preexisting relationship or association, either directly or through another person. You find warm recruits by creating lists of friends, family, and acquaintances. It also includes asking people that you know to put you in touch with their contacts that might be interested in your opportunity. These people that have networks that you can tap into are called "connectors", and they're an important part of your networking efforts.

Prospecting Methods

Now that you understand the two source types of recruits, let's talk about the methods for recruiting. These include networking, lacing, shoulder tapping, formal job fairs, opening your mouth everywhere, social media, and job boards.

Networking

So, what are the most productive sources and methods of recruiting? Should you focus on online ads? Spend one day a week at your local college campus? Call through everyone in your phone? Which method is best? Everyone I interviewed was unanimous on this subject—the most effective form of recruiting is networking. Here's why.

"Networking works because of two factors: trust and value. If you are recruiting through your network, trust will be high because the relationship is already there, which then makes building value in the opportunity easy."

Networking is to recruiting what referrals are to sales. Think back to the last time you received a referral text. It may have read something like, "Hey John, one of our friends is a customer of yours. They gave me your number and said they loved working with you and loved the system. We're interested in getting set up at our house and wanted to see when you could come by this week."

Having knocked doors for over a decade, I can say there is literally nothing better than receiving a text like that! You know that those leads have a near 100% chance of closing. Every door knocker knows the biggest obstacle to getting sales is building trust. If trust is already baked in, then it makes the sale so much easier. It's exactly the same with recruiting. When trust is baked in because the recruit has a relationship with you, they'll be more receptive to actually listen to your opportunity. Compared to recruits who are cold contacted, a higher percentage of warm recruits will meet, sign, and sell.

If networking is so effective, though, why don't more sales recruiters do it? It's because most recruiters greatly underestimate the size of their actual network and feel they don't have a big enough network to recruit from. This is absolutely false! I'm going to teach you a tool that changed the game of recruiting for me and countless other aspiring recruiters. If you understand and utilize it, you will soon find yourself with a vast quantity of qualified recruiting leads. The tool is called the "100 List" and it's something you need to use daily in your recruiting. Here's how one recruiter explains it.

*"If you feel like you don't have any recruiting leads,
then you don't understand the game of recruiting.
Every year I make a list of 100 people that I know.
I'll even put my mom, dad, cousin, uncle, teachers,
friends, everyone on that list. It doesn't mean that I'm
necessarily going to recruit those individuals, but I'm
going to use those individuals as systems of input that
I can pull from. Once I have that list, I start opening
up those networks and recruiting from them. From
those 100 people, I immediately gain a network of
potential recruits so large it'll keep me busy the entire
year."*

Your network includes every contact in your phone,
every friend on social media, and everyone that was
part of any group you ever belonged to, past or
present. Your network also includes everyone in each
of their networks! The 100 List opens up networks of
networks! By defining your network in this way, it
becomes obvious that it is truly infinitely large.

- Start to build your "100 List" by collecting all the
  contacts from all your networks into one place.
- Church

- School (kindergarten to college. Grab your year book!)
- Fraternities/Sororities
- Sports Teams
- Gaming Friends
- Social Media Contacts (All platforms)
- Contacts in your phone
- Any other source you can think of

Next, look through your network while asking the following two questions. "Who would do well in my opportunity?" And "Who would I love to work with?" Do not filter! As you look through your network to identify recruiting prospects, avoid pre-filtering people out with thoughts like, "Oh, he's too deep into his career, he'd never come do door-to-door" or "Oh, she sold before and hated it, she would never do it again." If you feel like they would do well, or you would want to work with them, put them on your 100 List.

Don't forget to include your connectors! Your general contractor Dad may not be a good candidate for your sales team, but he may have your next top rep hanging dry wall for him right now! Identify

connectors and use the following script to empower
them to help you recruit:

"Hey, I wanted to let you know I'm building out my
sales team. It would really help me out if you could
connect me with anyone you know that needs work
or is looking for a career change. I'm looking for
business-minded, hardworking, self-motivated
individuals that would be interested in making really
good money and expanding their skill set. Who do
you know that might be looking for an opportunity
like that? Will you keep me in mind in case you run
into someone who might be a good candidate?"

Next, look over your list and identify your top ten.
Ask yourself who would be the easiest people on the
list to recruit and who would be your dream recruits.
Circle those ten.

Then make a plan for each of them to get them to
take a recruiting meeting. For some, it may be as
simple as texting them and asking them to grab lunch
with you so you can tell them about the job. For
others, it may require a year of light social media
interaction, building up to a relationship, and finally,

a conversation about working together. Whatever it is, make a specific plan of attack for those ten individuals.

Now get to work! Take action immediately! Don't wait! Mel Robbins, author of the "The 5 Second Rule", explains that "If you have an instinct to act on a goal, you must physically move within 5 seconds or your brain will kill it. The moment you feel an instinct or a desire to act on a goal or a commitment, do it!" Approaching someone to recruit them can be nerve-racking. But the longer you wait to take action, the harder it will be to do so.

Once you've made plans of attack for those ten, repeat this process and identify the next top ten prospects. Repeat this process until you've worked through your 100 list. Work through your plan of action and create a new list every year or as often as needed to keep your pipeline full.

Lacing

Lastly, you'll want to utilize a powerful recruiting hack to maximize the 100 list. Remember that connectors can include friends, family, classmates, or anyone you know, but there is one type of Connector that reigns supreme! The top recruiters in door-to-door were all in total agreement that the most effective people to network through are your current recruits—this is called lacing, and here's why it's so effective.

"Lacing is the most powerful form of recruiting. You get more return for your effort because you're able to empower a growing leader. If you recruit through your current reps, then you have influence over a group instead of just an individual. If you can motivate a leader to rally their contacts to the opportunity, then all you really need to do is recruit a couple good leaders and you'll have a large team just like that."

When you recruit through Lacing, you double dip: You not only gain new recruits, but you also simultaneously build a future sales leader! You begin to leverage the power of exponential growth. Every professional recruiter I interviewed echoed this idea. Here's what three different recruiters said on this topic.

"Recruiters make the mistake of trying to do it all themselves. Empower the recruits you have to be leaders. When you're empowering your reps to manage teams, then you'll grow exponentially. You'll have ten people who are as passionate about it as you are. You will then literally become ten times as productive."

"It's all about empowering your people. If you do all the recruiting work for your reps, then you are really doing them a disservice. Make your reps do recruiting work because then you will turn everybody into recruiters. It's 100% empowerment."

"The best way to recruit is to make your current recruits successful and then they will recruit like crazy for you. I'll try to recruit people that have access to a great network. Social organizations like a fraternity or a church where a lot of people know each other. Those are by far the best sources of recruiting. But here's the thing I've found. It doesn't really work if you just cold contact these organizations and try to recruit everybody. You have to gain access to these groups organically through

100%
EMPOWERMENT

the other people you recruit. If you can do that, your organization will explode!"

Think about it. If you help ten of your reps make their own 100 lists, you'll have 1000 warm leads to recruit! So pause your reading right here and text your three best reps the following, "Hey, when are you free to meet up this week for an hour? I have a tool that I believe is going to help you recruit a ton of people. I want to show you how to use it to build your team. Just let me know when you can meet!"

Schedule time every week to meet with your reps and help them become successful recruiters. Engaging in this process will increase the likelihood of prospecting success, magnify your influence, and empower your people to grow and increase their earnings.

Now that you understand how to maximize your pool of warm contacts, let's talk about cold contact recruiting. If networking and lacing are the holy grails of recruiting, is there any even any reason to cold contact? Absolutely. There's three reasons that you should fish in the chilly waters of cold contact recruit prospecting.

First, cold contact recruiting is the most consistent method of prospecting. While networking and lacing are effective, they are not the most steady and stable. It's tough to build a system around networking that will fill your pipeline consistently. Again, it's like referrals. They're awesome and incredibly effective, but you can't always control when they come. What would happen if you tried to build your sales career exclusively off of referrals? You'd have a high close ratio, but low sales volume. It's the same with recruiting. Quality networks will vary in size. Also reps will vary in their willingness to recruit people they know. Cold contact recruiting offers a consistent, quantifiable, and measurable source of recruiting.

Second, cold contacting makes you more likely to actually do recruiting work. The more you cold contact prospect, the more you will appreciate networking and lacing, and so the more you will do it. It also consistently puts recruiting meetings on your calendar that forces you to do recruiting work.

And third, cold contact recruiting is what makes you a professional recruiter. No professional recruiter ever succeeded exclusively from warm contacts. You will never become or even feel like a professional recruiter unless you incorporate cold contact recruiting into your regiment.

Now that you know why cold contact recruiting is important, let's discuss how to do it. Because I didn't have a local network to recruit from, I was forced to figure out how to use these methods effectively. They consistently fed my recruiting pipeline for years, and they'll feed yours as well if you use them! Though shoulder tapping, opening your mouth everywhere, social media, and job boards, you'll find more recruits than you can handle!

Prospecting Methods

Shoulder Tapping

"Go now! Go now! They're under us! " About 50 miles off the California coast, I am jostled awake by our Skipper screaming that his fish finder is tagging a massive school of blue fin tuna 50' below the boat! I had fallen asleep in a bean bag on the boat deck, fully clothed from head to toe in wetsuit, mask, snorkel, weight belt, fins, and speargun. "Start your breath up and get in the water now!" Half awake, I start packing air into my lungs, barely getting my goggles on my face as I flip over the side of the boat. Whatever sleepiness I had left in my body disappeared the second I hit the chilly pacific water. I lay horizontally on the surface to catch a breath, but hear the Skipper again, "there's no time! Punch it now!" I flip upside down with my dive fins to the sky and begin my dive. I try to control my descent to preserve my air and reduce my heart rate. Twenty feet. Thirty feet. Forty feet. Fifty feet. Sixty feet. Finally, I see them. A school of shimmering, absolutely massive Tuna. As they circle, each one keeps a fixed gaze on me with their giant eye. Against my body, I hold a speargun as long as I am tall. I leveled out my body, stretched out the gun, line the spear up just behind the eye of the largest Tuna, and pulled the trigger.

Growing up in San Diego, I spent a lot of time in the ocean. More time than is possible without missing quite a bit of school! I got scuba certified at a young age, and spent my childhood under the water, exploring the reef, playing with fish, and collecting sea creatures, shells, and bottles. Recently I picked up a new ocean hobby, spearfishing! Spearfishing is hunting for fish. You catch fish with a speargun, which is essentially an underwater crossbow hooked together with a fishing line. You take a big breath, dive deep, and stalk the fish in their environment until you get one curious enough to take a shot. If you're skilled, you'll land a big fish and enjoy a delicious dinner!

Shoulder tapping refers to walking up to strangers in a predesignated location, tapping them on the shoulder or doing something else to get their attention, and pitching them on your opportunity. It's similar to spearfishing, which might be why it's my favorite way to recruit! I like it because like spearfishing, it's proactive. Instead of waiting around for recruits to randomly cross your path, you go find them in their environment!

It's incredibly effective and can be super fun! It's also unique in that the initial contact happens face-to-face with a prospect that fits a predetermined demographic. Just go wherever your ideal candidates are and talk to them! Go to malls or trade shows. Go to events where you'll find people that simply share a common interest with you. Are car enthusiasts at car shows ideal candidates for door-to-door sales? If you're a major car enthusiast, then definitely! Wherever you can find people that would do well in sales or that you can easily build a connection with, go there and talk to them. I'm going to focus this section on college campus shoulder tapping, because that's how I built my sales region. In between classes, I would approach students in the halls or that were sitting down eating and talk to them about sales. After I graduated, I continued to go to college campuses and recruit. I taught my reps how to do it as well, and we would go as a team to campus, post up at different spots, and shoulder tap. Here's some of the best practices I learned over my years of shoulder tapping.

The Approach

Whenever you shoulder tap someone, make sure you have something to hand them. Handing someone a card or flyer gives context for what's about to happen. If you just walk up to people and start asking questions or talking, they're going to be very confused and possibly put off. So as you are asking your initial question, hand them your card or flyer.

The first words out of your mouth should be a question. This will force the prospect to stop and engage. It depends on the situation, but in general the more fun, and less formal, the better. If you are handing them a flyer to a pizza party, ask a question related to the event: the games, the prizes, the food.

[hand flyer]
"Hey, do you play Xbox? Awesome, you want to win a free one?"
"Hey, do you play ping pong? Want to win prize money playing?"
"Do you like food? Awesome, come get some free food!"

Other questions to ask on a college campus:

"What are you studying?" (Figure out how they plan to get real-world experience related to their major and how sales will help.)

"Do you have an internship lined up yet?" (Position your sales jobs as a learning experience for their major. Some schools will even grant internship credit if you ask.)

"Have you received a scholarship yet?" (Consider setting up your own "scholarship" for student sales reps that hit certain sales levels.)

"What are you doing this summer?"
"When do you graduate?"
"Have you heard of [your company]?"
"Have you heard of [your industry]?"
"Have you heard of summer sales?"
"Where do you work?"

These are all amazing qualifying questions that will engage the student and give you a starting point for crafting your conversation. Now that you know how to start the conversation with a recruit, let's talk about how to end it.

Event–Based Recruiting

In Event Based Recruiting, you break the recruiting process down into key events or experiences that the recruit needs to have before they will sign. For example: initial contact, attend recruiting party, interview with the manager, attend team event, meet the owners, attend training, shadow someone knocking, sign. Each event progresses the recruit closer and closer to signing.

When you shoulder tap, you need to identify in advance what that next event is going to be. The two most effective events to recruit to in shoulder tapping are next-day interviews and pizza parties.

If you are running next-day interviews, your goal in shoulder tapping is to commit as many people as possible to meet with you for a job interview. If you are recruiting on campus, do the interviews on campus. This will make it easy for the recruits. Use the following close at the end of your initial shoulder tapping conversation.

"John, it was really good chatting with you. Based on what you've told me, I think you could be a good fit for our program. Out of every one hundred students we meet, we'll usually narrow that down to about ten that we bring on. Those ten will typically earn $X during the summer and get really good resume-building experience. I'd love for you to interview with us tomorrow here on campus. Are you here in the mornings or evenings? Awesome, I have times at 3:00 and 4:00, what time would work best for you. Great."

Stack your calendar and know in advance what the next event that you are recruiting them to is. Is it to come tour your company headquarters? To come to an orientation or training? To come meet the other reps they'll be working with. Whatever it is, know it ahead of time and commit them to that next event!

While next-day interviews are simple, throwing a fun event is much more effective! Recruiting to a fun event will yield a much higher turnout. If your event is awesome, people you committed to come will bring other people, maximizing the success of your efforts. Follow these tips to ensure maximum turnout and success.

Center your event either around a valuable or a fun experience. For value, host a keynote speaker on a topic that your demographic loves. Examples include starting a business while in school, making money in real estate or crypto, the true story of a young millionaire, etc. Bring the captain of one of the college teams or someone super wealthy in the community. Then raffle off prizes at the end.

If you are centering your event around fun, then host a tournament in ping pong, water pong, spikeball, eSports, bowling, or any other game your demographic likes or feels that they can win. Have awesome prizes like apple products, cash, gift cards to beloved restaurants, drones, gaming systems, etc.

Whatever format you choose, make sure there is free food, prizes, and awesome vibes! Invite all of your reps to attend. Even if they have no recruits, more bodies means more energy. It will look like tons of people are interested in your events and opportunity.

Make sure to capture all the info of everyone that attends! Have a QR that takes attendees to a form that collects their basic info. In order to get a raffle ticket or be entered to compete, they have to fill out the form.

After the keynote speaker finishes. Give a quick pitch to a now captive audience that connects whatever they just heard to your opportunity. For example, explain how working with your sales program will get them the cash they need to start investing. Or how competing in sales will help them compete in life. If you are hosting a tournament, round everyone up for a pitch before you start. Thank them for coming out, let them know it was made possible by [your company], and tell them quickly why your job is so awesome and how this event is proof. If you are organized, collect everyone's info upfront, pique interest with a quick pitch, have fun, and get to know people during the event, you will have a fresh new pool of very stoked recruiting leads to meet with!

Another way to drive attendance to your even is to post flyers on cars and even by knocking student housing the way you knock on doors. Keep an organized street sheet. Keep track of what apartments you knocked, and who you talked to. Try and find the influencers, the students that everyone knows, etc. Listen to how this recruiter approached recruiting with the same organized process as he did selling.

"Aspiring recruiters will often tell me they've already exhausted their network. Great! Then let's go create a new network. How do we do that? Well, where do you live? What is the closest campus to you? The nearest mall? What can be a consistent use of personal time that will bring you recruits? Let's section off this college apartment complex and treat it like a knocking area. I used to keep a three-ring binder labeled 'Recruiting' in my car. I'd knock college apartments with it, take notes, and treat it like a street sheet for selling. I'd write down who lives where, who does what, and who has influence. I'd pay people $20 to introduce me to the most influential individuals in the complex. I just did whatever was necessary to get face-to-face with someone I could recruit. Just do whatever it takes to get yourself in front of potential recruits!"

One caveat. College campuses are a precious resource for recruiting. Don't poison the pool by getting banned from the school. Be respectful in all of your communication with the college and follow all their guidelines. They are very protective of their students and it's very easy to get kicked out permanently!

Formal Job Fairs

Another awesome way to get great shoulder tapping is through formal job fairs. These events strengthen your relationship with the colleges because they are typically paid events that bring in revenue for the schools. It's also an opportunity for them to get to know your company and for you to meet the school's faculty. Additionally, the students attending a job fair are actively looking for work and are even better qualified than students you find cold contacting. Schedule as many fruitful formal recruiting events as you can.

Always make sure to have the absolute best booth out of all the companies. This includes a tablecloth, two pop-up banners on the side, a large pop up backdrop, a cooler with energy drinks, tons of freebies like ChapStick, pens, hand sanitizer, frisbees, squishy balls, candy, etc., a tv with a video loop showing all the awesome trips and incentives your company does, and a sheet or form to put in their information to learn more. Make sure that when someone walks into the career fair, it's obvious that your company is the one dominating.

To recap, shoulder tapping is fun and easy. You can do it today! Just grab some business cards, pick a spot, walk up to someone, and ask one of the questions listed above. Don't delay because you don't have your whole recruiting pitch mapped out. You'll figure it out as you go. And if you burn through a couple of attempts trying to figure it out, who cares! It's like the doors. Sent is better than perfect. Just get started!

Opening Your Mouth Everywhere

Another extremely effective way to cold contact recruit is to just infuse recruiting into your lifestyle and talk about your opportunity with everyone you meet. The best recruiters don't treat recruiting like a 9-5 job. Recruiting is a part of their identity and brand. As a result, they never miss an opportunity to recruit. Some of the best door-to-door reps were recruited through chance meetings by a recruiter that had made a habit of opening their mouth everywhere. Listen to how this recruiter described it.

"Recruiting has to be something that you implement in your everyday life. When you go get your oil changed, you give your card to the person at the counter, and you try and recruit them. When you're at the mall buying Christmas presents, you try and recruit everybody you talk to. When you're getting your new cell phone, recruit the sales rep. If I'm at home depot with my wife, I'm trying to recruit the person that's showing me which piece of PVC pipe to buy. It's great to recruit at a booth or a scheduled event, but more importantly, I'm constantly trying to recruit everybody I come into contact with as I'm living my life. It allows me to talk to a lot more people. It's more efficient. Recruit while you're just living life."

This recruiter sums it up perfectly.

"The best source of recruiting, in my opinion, is everywhere, all the time. Always actively open your mouth and express what the opportunity is"

Where and when should you are recruiting? Everywhere and all the time!

Social Media

One morning I woke up to the following direct message in Instagram.

"Hey Adam, you don't know me, but I've been following you for a while. First, I just wanted to say thanks for the value you put out there. It's helped me a ton the past couple years. I wanted to reach out cause I'm not exactly stoked where I'm at right now, and I see you guys crushing it over there. Are you free to hop on a call sometime this week?"

If shoulder tapping is like spearfishing, recruiting through social media is like fishing with a fishing pole. It takes patience and consistent effort keeping your line in the water, but it's incredibly effective. You could also think of recruiting on social media like planting a seed that you water, keep in the light, and nurture as it grows.

Below are four pro tips for effectively recruiting through social media.

Be Authentic. Make a list of individuals you want to work with, but don't direct message them and try and recruit them. Instead, like and comment on their content. Interact back and forth with them for a while. Let the seed of the relationship grow. Don't try and harvest before it's planted. For some, you may be able to just ask for a meeting up front, but most will require nurturing first. Personally, I don't like sending super direct recruiting messages. To me, this would be akin to planting a seed, and then drowning it in water, hoping that it grows faster. You'll just end up killing it. Or trying to smack a fish in the head with your hook and hope it catches. I like organically interacting with people in an authentic way. I regularly hop on and like or comment on the content of people I want to work with. I congratulate their successes, laugh at funny content they post, ask questions, and engage in a convo, none of which has anything to do with sales or recruiting. I know that in time, they will be seeking a new career or new leadership, and the work I put into building a relationship will put me top of mind for their next career move.

Give. Don't just take, give. Create, or at a minimum, redistribute valuable content. Repost inspirational quotes or stories, funny memes, educational articles, tips, and hacks. Try to create your own content. People love authenticity. Get over the feeling of being embarrassed, record yourself explaining something valuable, and post it. Sent is better than perfect. Don't stress too hard, just get started with whatever you've got and build up from there. The idea is to establish yourself online as a person of value.

Follow. Follow as many people that match the demographic of your ideal recruit as possible. Follow everyone that follows other sales companies. Follow fraternity or sorority members at your local college. Connect with people on LinkedIn. On Instagram you can search for hashtags. This will display any post where the person that made the post used the hashtag. What hashtags are your ideal recruits using? Search things like #doortodoor, #entrepreneurship, #solar, #sales, etc. Type the name of a company that employs sales reps in the LinkedIn search bar. Then click "People", then "Locations", then filter by your location. This will show you sales reps in your area. Dm them and ask how long they've done sales. Have an organic conversation that includes qualifying questions to see if they're happy with their situation. Put as many lines in the water as you can and get as many people as you possibly can following you, seeing you, and benefiting from what you put out.

Be Patient. In time you will see recruiting conversations and relationships sprout up organically. If you do it right, you won't even be the one reaching out. Potential recruits will message you and ask what you do, how you like it, and if they can get information about it.

Job Boards

Posting ads to job sites is an effective way to create a consistent funnel of candidates. Use job sites like

Indeed, Facebook, and LinkedIn to market for recruits. This method of prospecting typically produces a high volume and lower quality candidates because you are not hand selecting them. Anyone on the internet can apply. This means it's important to prescreen applicants before they can schedule an interview with you. Require applicants watch a quick video and fill out a form that makes it clear you are hiring for a door-to-door sales position. When candidates do schedule, don't just hop on a zoom with them from your car in a tee shirt. Make it a professional experience. Create a formal hiring process that includes prescreening, multiple interviews, and a formal job offer.

Run your final interviews immediately before or during your sales meetings so the candidate can see your team and culture in person. If the interview load becomes excessive, empower your future leaders to conduct interviews.

In conclusion, through networking, lacing, shoulder tapping, opening your mouth everywhere, utilizing social media, and posting on job boards, you will recruit more people than you can handle. All recruiters have all these recruiting sources available to them. So why do such a high percentage of aspiring recruiters fail? It's not due to a lack of opportunity or resources, but due to a lack of effort. The final and most important source of recruiting, is simple effort.

Mandatory Minimum Effort

Most recruiters simply do not apply enough effort to their recruiting endeavors to make them successful. To prove this, reflect on your experiences knocking on doors and consider how they might apply to recruiting. Here's how one recruiter put it.

"Think of how many accounts you sold last year. How many people did you have to talk to, to sell that amount? How many doors total did you have to knock? Now think about recruiting. How many people did you try and recruit last year? How many people did you honestly sit down with? When you compare your selling effort to your recruiting effort, the gap becomes real. It takes the same or even a higher volume of prospects to find a hit. As effective as networking is, at the end of the day, it doesn't

really matter where you look because you can find people everywhere. The bottom line is that in order to be a good recruiter, you need lots of practice. You need to get in front of a lot of people. You need a large volume of experience. You need to be setting up meetings with a lot of people so that it becomes a skill set. "

Consider how a recruiting routine could give you predictable results in the same way your selling routine gives you predictable sales.

"Think of selling. Selling is so simple because you know the hours you're working, and you have a developed system for knocking. You know how many prospects you need to talk to each day. You scale that average and execute it over a week, month, a year. You win because you put the numbers game in your favor. But for some reason, people forget this rule of prospecting when they recruit. They just stick their finger in the air and hope that somebody comes across their plate. They have no structure, no system,

Common sense is not always common practice.

MANDATORY

MINIMUM

EFFORT

no schedule for recruiting. Then they get frustrated that they don't recruit. It's just common sense that if you talk to more people, you're going to recruit more people. But then again, common sense is not always common practice."

Ramping up your prospecting to the level required to be a successful professional recruiter starts with a change of mindset. Remember your commitment at the start of this book to be willing to let go of some preconceived notions about recruiting? One false notion that aspiring recruiters hold is that they can achieve the same success in recruiting that they've experienced in sales, but without putting the same effort into recruiting that they put into sales.

You need to embrace being a rookie again. Most reps sell for a while before they start recruiting. This means that most rookie recruiters are experienced sales reps. They already went through the uncomfortable and difficult learning curve of sales. They already experienced having a knot in their stomach before a pitch and feeling like they don't know what they're doing. And they don't want to repeat that experience. So they avoid recruiting. Do you remember the commitment you made before you started reading this chapter? You committed that you were willing to embrace discomfort and difficulty in the pursuit of becoming a professional recruiter. Most recruiters fail this test. Read this statement and consider how the scrappy "just get it done" work ethic you use in sales should be applied in your recruiting.

"Once you feel like you've worked through your network, then the grind of recruiting really starts. This is where it's time to roll up your sleeves and say, 'let's go get it done'. Go make 100 cold contacts. Go hold an event somewhere. Go anywhere! So many people are willing to drive to some other state on a sales trip, so why aren't you willing to drive out there to hit up a school? Go hit up all the cell phone stores and find recruits! Go hit the mall in the middle of the day and look for opportunities. Don't be afraid to get your butt kicked. However, you've got to get it done in recruiting, you've just got to get it done. Sales reps are always willing to go out and bust their butt and knock on 100 doors to get one sale every day. And that's a great one-time income. But why not go talk to 100 different potential recruits and get one that will

*bring you a recurring source of income? Maybe
you're afraid to fail because you've failed before. Do
you allow the fear of failure to stop you from selling?
No? Then why is recruiting any different?"*

If the picture isn't clear yet, this should sum it up
perfectly:

*"The best source of recruiting? It's effort. The source
is not as important as putting in a hard enough hustle
to make it work. No matter
how you do it, nothing is
going to happen without
action. At the end of the
day, it really just comes
down to desire and grit."*

Whats the
best source
of recruiting?

EFFORT.

So which prospect pool should you attack- warm or
cold? Which methods should you use? The answer is
all of them! It's necessary to learn and work all
sources and methods of recruiting in order to get
enough prospects into your recruiting pipeline to
succeed. To understand this better, let's analyze the
math behind your recruiting funnel. We've discussed

the sources and methods of recruiting, now let's discuss the metrics.

The Averages Of Recruiting

Business management consultant Jim Rohn taught that if you do something often enough, then ratios will begin to appear. For example, if you shoot a basketball from the three-point line enough times, then eventually, you will know your shooting average and can predict how many baskets you will make in the future. For your business, these averages can be used to create systems that will deliver predictable results. In sales, we know this principle as the Law Of Averages. If you're not familiar with the Law of Averages, it works like this.

An effective door knocker knows that if, for example, they knock on 100 doors, then they'll talk to 50 homeowners, schedule 25 appointments, do 10 presentations, and close 5. They can work backward from their goal and know what input they need to reach it. Just like in sales (remember sales and recruiting are the same!), in order to be an effective recruiter you must know your averages.

While the averages for your recruiting funnel will vary based on the source, method and skill, The Law Of Halves is a power formula that will ensure recruiting success. Using this formula will deliver results that are at least as good as what you expect, and likely much better.

The Law Of Halves: Half of your recruits will fall out at each step of the recruiting pipeline.

This recruiter explains.

"I've found that if I approach 100 people, I can get 50 to sit down with me. After the interview process, I get 25 of those to sign. When I get those 25 out on the doors to try it out, I can get about 12 to actually stick it out. Then of those, 6 will finish the sales season and come back next year."

Now let's do some math. Using these averages, we can create a formula that will allow us to work backward and know exactly how many prospective recruits we need to contact in order to build the sales team that we want. If there are four steps in the recruiting funnel before we get a solid and committed rep, and we assume that half the recruits will drop out at each step, then we can just take our goal of committed reps and multiple it by 16 to figure out how many people we need to contact about the opportunity. Let's demonstrate with an example.

Suppose you want to build a 50-person sales team. If you want 50 committed reps, then you need to have 100 people start your sales program because half the people that start will fall off. That means you need to sign 200 reps because half the people that sign will quit before they even start. That means you need to give 400 hiring presentations because half the people you meet with won't sign. That means you need to pitch 800 people on meeting with you because half the people you ask will say no. Follow the law of halves, and you'll get your 50 solid and committed reps!

Does contacting 800 people make you feel a little queasy? If so, skip ahead and read Recruiting Sin #3 in Chapter 7: Underestimating the Amount of Work Required to Succeed at Recruiting. Also remember the commitment you made at the start of this book to

The Law of Halves

100 Contacts

50 Presentations

25 Signed

12 Start

6 Solid

Half of your prospects will fall out at every step in the recruiting process escalate your work ethic to painful levels. Realistically though, if you've read and understand the preceding section on the sources and methods of prospecting, then it should be obvious that with a proper schedule and effort, making 800 recruiting contacts is an easily manageable task especially if you empower your people to help in the effort!

The law of half is more of a safety net and a guideline that it is a law. Your recruiting metrics and conversion ratios will vary by method (for example, your metrics will be much better with warm networking than cold contacting), but it's important to properly set expectations and know what inputs are necessary in order to achieve the outputs you want.

It's also important to know the averages of recruiting because the biggest mistake aspiring recruiters make is that they don't recruit! Meaning they don't drive enough potential recruits into the recruiting funnel to see the success they want on the other side.

Recruiters often look at their numbers and conclude that they are failing, but the reality is that most of these "failures" are not failures at all. The recruiter is actually doing their job correctly but just not on a big enough scale. They fall short because they don't understand the averages of recruiting and are not putting in enough work to bring in enough prospects. After years of mentoring aspiring recruiters, this leader describes the way that most new recruiters don't give a strong enough effort to succeed.

"Recruiters underestimate how much work they have to put in to recruit a proper team. Honestly, it's incredible how many people you need to talk to. I don't think most recruiters are prepared for it. My own managers will come to me freaking out and say, 'All my reps dropped out!' I say let me see your stats really quick. How many people have you signed this year? They say ten people, but only four have stuck. I say okay, cool, well, your stats are as good as mine. You're just not reaching out to enough people."

Learn and apply The Laws Of Halves and The Law of 16 to ensure that you are getting enough recruiting action to succeed as a professional recruiter.

Putting It Into Action

Let's say you're a third-year door-to-door rep with a couple of other reps you randomly recruited along the way. You want to grow a strong sales office with 30 super committed reps that plan to work in your program for years to come. Using The Law of 16, you know that you need to contact 480 people about the job. You then look at your prospecting sources and methods list.

Now you're going to make a plan, including a schedule that will allow you to hit these goals. You look over your sources and methods of prospecting: Networking, Lacing, Shoulder Tapping, Opening My Mouth Everywhere, Social Media, Job Boards.

You block out two hours every Monday to work on yours and your recruit's 100 list. You block out three hours every Tuesday for shoulder tapping and recruiting events. Tuesday nights, you schedule a standing team hangout which makes it easy for your reps to bring friends and contacts. You create a social media account for your sales team that highlights your culture and success. You put up job postings online and empower your two top reps to conduct interviews. As long as you're consistent and leverage your reps by getting them stoked to recruit, you should easily be able to make 3 contacts per day and sign one person per day.

Chapter Two
PROSPECTING
Summary & Action Items

- Sources: Prospects fall into two buckets, cold and warm contacts.

- Methods: Utilize Networking, Lacing, Shoulder Tapping, Opening Your Mouth Everywhere, Social Media, and Job Boards to find prospects.

- Averages: Create a recruiting plan of action based on the Law of Halves and The Law of Sixteen.

- Remember, while warm prospecting is more effective, you must pair it with cold contacting in order to realize your recruiting potential.

- Focus your recruiting efforts on helping your current reps recruit. By lacing, you will grow your downline and develop your people at the same time.

- None of the methods are effective if you don't put in the work. Don't stress about the details. Just get started anywhere with anyone and don't stop.

What should you do right now?

- Fill out the 100 List found at the back of this book. Expand your network.

- Schedule a meeting with your current reps to begin empowering them to recruit.

- Fill every gap in your schedule with cold contacting opportunities.

- Crystalize that commitment you made to ramp up your work ethic to a level that feels painful.

- Read Sin Number 3 under "The Deadly Sins of Recruiting."

- Read "The 10X Rule" by Grant Cardone.

Imagine having a week stacked with so many solid recruiting appointments that you barely have time for them all. Recruiting and fun may seem like opposite experiences, but that's only because you haven't done it enough. Grant Cardone explains how even the most tedious task can become a passion.

"Most people only work enough so that it feels like work, whereas successful people work at a pace that gets such satisfying results that work is a reward. Truly successful people don't even call it work; for them, it's a passion. Why? Because they do enough to win!"

If you follow the guidelines in this chapter to the degree indicated, recruiting will become your passion. You will, without question, achieve the volume of recruiting success necessary to charge toward a seven-figure income. And you will enjoy and love every second of it.

Now that you understand what it takes to fill your pipeline with potential recruits, let's discuss how to know which recruits are the best fits for your opportunity.

Chapter Three
QUALIFYING
How to know when you've found top talent.

In 1577, Sir Martin Frobisher returned to England from a mining expedition in Canada. His excitement about the gold he found piqued the Queen's interest enough that she sent him back the following year, fully funded with ships, supplies, and men. At phenomenal cost, Sir Martin shipped 2.8 million pounds of the material he had discovered back to England. Upon analysis, it was discovered that what he had found was a mineral known as pyrite or fool's gold!

Sir Martin's massive failure was rooted in the fact that he did not know how to properly identify the gold he sought. This failure was a career ender for Martin!

Many ambitious and dedicated recruiters have also unintentionally ended their own recruiting careers by not knowing what to look for. They invest time, money, and energy into what may look like golden recruits, only to discover too late that they invested their resources in fool's gold! Hiring and investing in the wrong people will suck the life and joy out of recruiting. Bad experiences like these are often enough to cause hopeful recruiters to abandon their quest entirely.

Just like in sales, qualifying is the ability to identify which prospective recruits are great fits for your opportunity. It is also the process of determining how your opportunity best meets a recruit's needs. It is an absolutely critical skill that all professional recruiters must possess.

What To Look For In Recruits

Critical Personality Traits

In order for recruits to qualify for your sales program, they must exhibit three attributes. Specifically, they must be hard working, coachable, and positive. If they possess these qualities, then they are great candidates, even if they lack sales ability. If they don't possess these qualities, they're bad fits, even if they're incredibly talented salespeople!

Hard Working

I once recruited someone with mediocre communication skill. His sales volume bounced between highs and lows, and so did his paychecks. The difficulties of selling door-to-door and commission-based pay messed with his head A LOT, and he found it hard to consistently succeed. His first year with me, he was the lowest performing rep in my region, and one of the worst in the company. But this rep worked hard. It was common for him to be out knocking on doors late into the night and long after the rest of the office had already made it home for the day

Even though he wasn't the most naturally talented sales rep, his superior work ethic eventually translated to superior sales ability. His unrivaled work ethic led to unrivaled performance. His hustle fueled his success, his success fueled his confidence, his confidence further fueled his work ethic, and the virtuous cycle continued until this rep became the number one rep in the entire company, breaking industry records in the process.

Of all the attributes I look for in a new recruit, work ethic is number one. It is not only the most important for sales success but also the hardest to teach. After recruiting for over a decade, I've learned to pick the untalented hard worker every single time over the lazy all-star. Hard work acts like a great equalizer, allowing even the most disadvantaged and untalented recruits to eventually dominate. It also acts as a great debilitator, preventing even the most talented recruits from ever achieving their potential if they refuse to work.

When I'm qualifying a potential recruit, I want to know that they have a track record of forcing themselves to do hard things that they don't want to do. Or, if they are young and haven't had that opportunity, I want to know that they see value in and are excited about the fact that door-to-door sales are extremely difficult.

To figure out if a candidate possesses a good enough work ethic, ask qualifying questions like:

"What's the single hardest thing you've ever had to do in your life?"

"Can you give me examples of some really hard things you have done before?"

"What experiences in your life have prepared you for the difficulties of door-to-door sales?"

In setting expectations for how hard door-to-door sales is, I like to use a technique called "talk them out of it, talk them into it." The technique consists of painting the grimmest picture of door-to-door sales as possible. Talk about the difficulty, talk about the stress, talk about the risk of working and not making sales. Make it so that if someone were observing your recruiting presentation, they would think your job was to convince people not to do door-to-door sales! Then after you have set expectations, talk them "back into it" by gushing about how incredible the job is. For example:

"John, I want to be honest with you, door-to-door is likely going to be the hardest thing you've ever done. It's not just physically exhausting walking around all day, but also mentally and emotionally exhausting. People are going to push your buttons and get under your skin. You're going to fail a lot. In fact, most of your time is going to be spent getting rejected. You're going to feel like a failure, feel confused sometimes that you're not performing better, and feel frustrated. A lot of people that start out really excited to do this job wind up quitting. But the job is also amazing. If you stick it out, you'll hit personal development milestones you never dreamed possible for your life. You'll make more money than you've ever made in your life. You'll get incredible mentorship and coaching. You'll learn things about business and life that you'll be able to take with you to your other jobs or businesses you start. You'll get to change people's lives with our product. And in the process, it'll change your life."

Again, your goal is to set expectations and read how they respond to the idea of doing something hard. Does it get them excited? Do they feel driven to rise to the challenge? Are they committed to being one of the few who makes it? Or are they turned off by the difficulty?

Ask great qualifying questions and use "Talk them out of it, talk them into it" and you'll be able to successfully test the work ethic of a particular recruit.

Positive Attitude

A University once sent me one of their top athletes as part of a recruiting program I had set up with them. We hired him on the recommendation of his coach without an interview. He flew out to our sales territory to begin training. Our first door we knocked together was a miss. The homeowner cut me off rudely mid-sentence and slammed the door. As soon as the door shut, this athlete made a nasty comment about what an idiot the homeowner was. We continued knocking, running into a few other less than friendly people. Every single one of them got under his skin. After about twenty doors, he was fuming mad.

I explained the value of having tough skin and trying to find something positive in every negative situation. Despite the pep talk, he couldn't help himself from complaining about every person we talked to, about how hot it was, and about how stupid people were in general. We eventually pulled a sale out at the very end of the day. I tried to frame the day in the victory of our sale, but on the car ride home, he just complained about all the people we didn't sell. He also somehow found time to complain about his college classes and even his coach. His second day, I dropped him off to knock on some doors on his own and try the pitch out. I checked in after a couple of hours to see how he was doing. He let me know that I had given him crappy area and that no one was interested. He also explained that knocking on doors wasn't effective, and I would make way more money if I tried alternative marketing methods like flyers or online ads. I thanked him for his input. Even when this rep had positive experiences on the doors, he still managed to just focus on the negative.

I eventually talked to him about it and asked if he had ever noticed or considered that his experiences were not actually as bad as he was making them out to be in his mind. I asked him to consider if choosing to adopt a positive mindset, especially in the face of negative situations, would benefit him. He dismissed the notion and described himself as a "realist" who just "told it like it was." It became clear to me in time that this rep's negative mindset would prevent him from ever succeeding at the job. No amount of skill or work ethic could offset his negative mindset enough to allow him to be successful.

In addition, because misery loves company, he would often regale his negative tales to other rookies and reps in the office, spreading a culture of negativity and complaining. After multiple conversations, it became clear that he wasn't willing to let go of his negative mindset, and so I had to let him go. He went back to his hometown and I assume complained to his coaches about how terrible the experience was.

This is a cautionary tale. Don't foster stinking thinking! Be on the lookout for negative people. Negativity is a cancer that will spread throughout your entire team if you do not cut it out! Take special care to never introduce it to your program.

Similar to hard work, I'll take the untalented but positive recruit over the negative all-star every single

Who to Hire?

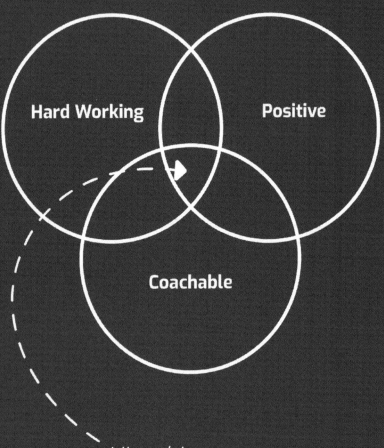

Hard Working

Positive

Coachable

Hire this person

time. In fact, there's no amount of sales volume that a negative recruit could bring that would outweigh the damage that they do to your program. Negativity is particularly damaging because it spreads like a virus. A high performing, but negative sales rep will always do more damage than harm. Quarantining negativity once it's introduced to your system is near impossible, so don't ever let it in!

To figure out if a candidate possesses a positive mindset, ask qualifying questions like:

"Why'd you leave your last job?"

"What kind of things bother you or get under your skin?"

"How do you usually respond to stress?"

If a recruit has a tendency to get triggered easily into a negative mindset, see if you can get them to do it during the interview. Observe what kind of things bug them, how easily they switched to negativity mode, and how intense that negativity is.

Coachable

I remember an interview I conducted with a prospective recruit. The recruit was so eager to prove how knowledgeable he was that he would repeatedly interrupt me and attempt to finish my sentences. It was as though he needed to constantly reassure himself that he already knew whatever I was trying to explain. This was annoying, but not enough that I didn't hire him. As he began his training, however, the behavior continued. In between doors, as I attempted to teach and explain things to him, it became obvious that he was not really listening. Instead, he was only thinking of how he could respond in a way that made it appear that he already knew what I was trying to teach. Eventually, it became intolerable, and I had to explain to the rep what he was doing and how it was hindering his training.

He understood and stopped interrupting, but his attitude didn't stop. He still felt as if he knew more than all his peers and trainers. He still perceived attempts to coach, train, and mentor him as insults to his intelligence and skills. And so he never learned to sell effectively. He stayed stagnant, and eventually, I had to send him home.

The third most important attribute to look for in a golden recruit is coachability. If someone, even unintentionally, refuses to accept coaching, mentoring, and training, they're going to fail and waste a lot of your time in the process. Additionally, these individuals will resist adapting to your culture, which is incredibly detrimental to your program.

To learn if someone is coachable, ask questions like:

"What do you hope to learn from this experience?"

"What have been some of the most important things you've learned over the last few years?"

"If you had to abandon some old habits or attitudes to fit into our culture, would you be ok with that?"

Critical Personality Traits Summary

To recap, you want to work with people who are not afraid to work hard, people who ooze positivity, and people that are excited to learn and become better.

These attributes correlate so closely to sales and general success that you should hire individuals with these characteristics, even if they seem below average in actual job competency or performance. As long as they possess these three characteristics, you can be confident that they can succeed.

You must run all prospects through this qualifying filter. Lazy, negative, know-it-all types are poison and will spread their bad habits and bad attitude through your organization like a disease, killing it from the inside out. It doesn't matter how much performance capacity they have, if they fail this test, they are out. Carefully vet prospects to ensure they possess these attributes.

As you qualify recruits, though, be careful not to "over-screen" and filter out people based on factors outside of these three. Sometimes recruiters go too far and mistakenly add other unnecessary filters. They allow discriminatory biases to steer them away from good people. For example, a recruiter that has only ever worked in offices comprised entirely of men may inadvertently assume that a female recruit is not as good of a candidate for the opportunity. I've known recruiters who only hired physically attractive people. Or recruiters who only hire sports stars. I've also known state champion athletes who quit their first day of knocking because they couldn't handle the rejection. And I've known oddball computer nerds who lead the company in performance. The opportunity to sell is for everyone, and everyone can dominate in sales. (Except lazy, negative people of course!) Over-screening is a massive mistake. If an individual proves to be hard-working, coachable, and positive, it's important to give them a fair shot. Let people surprise you! Listen to this recruiter's experience with misjudging people.

"Too many recruiters make the mistake of trying to recruit one certain type of person. I've learned not to

DON'T JUDGE

judge anybody. Often the people my instincts told me were not going to be good, turned out to be great. And sometimes, the people I thought were going to be great, completely flopped. I've learned to do my best to offer the opportunity to everyone. I always give my best training effort to everyone. I try and become everyone's friend. Some reps work out, and some don't but I'm not clairvoyant enough to know which ones will and which ones won't. Sometimes it's the most unlikely people that turn out to be the best at this. I promise everybody that works for me that I will give them at least as good of an opportunity, if not a better opportunity, than the one I had."

Rookies vs. Vets: Which Is Better?

When recruiting, also factor in a prospect's industry experience in determining the quality of a recruit. Veterans are defined as sales reps with over a year of door-to-door experience. Rookies are brand new to the job.

Which is better, veterans or rookies? Most recruiters assume the more experienced rep is better because

they don't need training and require less time and
attention. There are other factors to consider,
however. Read each of the following questions and
ask yourself which rep would be better.

Rookie vs. Vet

Which requires more training?
Which requires more work?
Which is more likely to demonstrate loyalty to you
and your program over time?
Which is more likely to be coachable?
Which is more likely to adapt to your culture?
Which will have better margins (be more profitable)?
Which will make you more money in the short run?
Which will make you more money in the long term?
Which will produce more in the short term?
Which will produce more in the long term?

As you thought through these questions, it should
become obvious that neither one is good or bad, just
different. Effective recruiters and sales leaders
understand these differences and how to properly mix
veterans and rookies into their program for maximum
success.

Generally speaking, the longer a recruiter or sales leader succeeds in door-to-door sales, the more they will come to appreciate and prefer rookies. Here's one recruiter's perspective.

"I'm not interested in any experienced sales reps. Honestly, hiring someone who has experience with another company in our industry is the biggest headache I've ever had. We go after rookies. It's a lot more work on the front end to recruit somebody from scratch and to program them to your system, but it's worth it."

Generally speaking, building with rookies will be much more work than recruiting vets. The benefits are worth it, though. Rookies are more likely to be optimistic sponges, grateful for any coaching they can get, and forever loyal to the people and company that brought them into the opportunity. Recruiting a veteran can sometimes be like adopting a teenager. To some degree, they're just going to come baked with their own perspectives and ways of doing things. These are obviously generalizations; some of the biggest hiring mistakes I've ever made were rookies, and some of the best recruits I've ever had were vets. Some vets are extremely grateful, loyal, and profitable, and some rookies are negative prima donnas. But generally speaking, you need to be aware of the differences and be intentional in prioritizing rookies. This doesn't mean you turn away vets, it just means you also need to be recruiting enough rookies to maintain a healthy balance on your team.

Use the Law of Rookie Growth and the Law of Veteran Demise to guide you in making sure you are building a healthy sales program that is poised for growth.

The Law of Rookie Growth

Rookie Production > 60% of Total Production = Growing Program

At least 60% of your production needs to come from rookies, or your team or company isn't going to grow. For example, if only 40% of last year's production came from rookies, it is unlikely you will experience good growth this year.

The Law of Veteran Demise

Veteran Production > 80% of Total Production = Dying Program

If 80% or more of your production comes from veterans, your program is in serious trouble. Do not get anywhere near this number! It just isn't possible to build your culture and grow with a mix that is that vet heavy. A sales program primarily made up of tenured vets is one that is doomed for stagnation. It's also not possible to truly craft your culture with that many veterans.

Take a moment to evaluate your recruiting pipeline and team. What percentage of your recruits are veterans? If it's over 50%, begin immediately to pump more rookies into the funnel. Be willing to take on the hard work of recruiting and building rookies.

Chapter Three
QUALIFYING
Summary & Action Items

- Look for people who can prove they possess a solid work ethic, coach-ability, and a positive attitude.

- Don't over screen. Give everyone a fair shot as long as they possess these attributes.

- Recruit everyone but prioritize rookies and do the hard work of people building.

Rookie Production > 60% of Total Production = Growing Program

Veteran Production > 80% of Total Production = Dying Program

What questions will you ask in your next interview to gauge a recruit's work ethic, coachability, and attitude?

What red flags would indicate that a recruit is lacking one or more of these attributes?

What subconscious biases have you held that would cause you to filter out a potentially good recruit? (Be honest! Everybody has them!)

Make a pros and cons list of hiring and training a rookie vs. a vet. Decide for yourself if it's worth it to focus on rookies.

Rookies   **Vets**

Pros: Pros:

Cons: Cons:

What percentage of your sales last year or quarter came from rookies, and what percentage came from vets?

Rookies: %_____

Vets: %_____

What does this mean you need to do?

By applying the techniques taught in this chapter, you will have truckloads of qualified recruits ready to be persuaded that your opportunity is the best one for them. The next chapter will teach you how to communicate your opportunity in a way that will cause recruits to flock to your program!

Chapter Four

PRESENTING

How do I get people absolutely stoked about my opportunity?

If done correctly, the recruiting presentation is magical. It's where the awesomeness of your opportunity clicks and where emotional energy is transferred. Following are the principles and practices that the best recruiters in door-to-door use to consistently and predictably take potential recruits from vaguely interested to absolutely stoked and committed. By building a relationship of trust, focusing on the long-term opportunity, and using stories, you will be able to dramatically improve your recruiting presentation skills.

Presenting Practice Number 1
Build a Relationship of Trust

After almost a year of construction, my backyard half pipe was complete. Four thousand epic square feet of awesomeness! I invited a bunch of buddies over to skate. Word of the epicness of my half pipe had spread, and a small group of friends quickly turned into a large crowd of strangers! I wound up meeting a bunch of rad people, one of whom worked in door-to-door selling pest control. We started talking shop. Because we shared a common love for an obscure sport, we got to know each other well. I got to know him professionally too. I learned about his history in the industry, what his long-term goals were, and what type of people he liked to work with. I discovered that he had actually interviewed with my company multiple times but had never joined because he didn't feel like the recruiters were a fit for him. As I got to know this individual better and better, the way to recruit him became more and more obvious. When we started having recruiting conversations, I was able to pair his wants and needs with my sales program so effectively that joining my team was an incredibly easy decision for him. Where other recruiters had failed, I had succeeded. You don't need to get to know someone for months before you can effectively recruit them. If you follow the steps below, you can create the same effect in just one meeting! I've learned that the initial recruiting meeting is really just a simple five-step process. Memorize these steps so that you can execute them in your next interview or recruiting presentation.

Step 1- Get to know the recruit.
Step 2- Get to know the recruit.
Step 3- Get to know the recruit.
Step 4- Get to know the recruit.
Step 5- Connect what you learned about them to what your opportunity offers.

Every recruiter I interviewed talked about the importance of building a relationship of trust in the presenting process.

"The first part is just getting to know them. Where are they from, what do their parents do, how many brothers and sisters do they have, what are they studying in college? Try and find some common

ground. I've found the more I get to know the recruit,
the greater the level of influence I have on them."

Here's how another recruiter put it.

"Spend the first 30-40 minutes just getting to know
the recruit and finding common ground. Ask them
what they know about the job and who they know that
does it. Then connect it all together."

Recruiting stems naturally from the relationship.
Listen to how these six different recruiters explain it.

"It's all about building a relationship of trust. I really
try to get to know the recruit I'm sitting down with.
Their likes and dislikes. I show them that I'm genuine
and normal. I want people to understand that I care
about them and that I want to know how I can help
them. So, I ask them, 'What are your goals for the
next year? How do you see yourself getting there?
How can our company help you get there? How can I
personally help you achieve your goals? What's your
three-year plan? What would have to happen for you
to feel like working here was a success?' That's my
process. I build a relationship of trust, I try to get an

idea of their goals, and I help them see how my opportunity can get them there."

"I focus on the recruit. I ask them about their past experience, their background, where they're from, what their needs are, and what they're looking for from the job. Once I know them on a deeper level, I just connect the opportunity to their situation."

"Really seek to understand where the recruit wants to go, what their goals are, and what they want to accomplish in life. Only then can you match those goals with what your program offers. If you approach recruiting this way, it really is a pretty simple process. Too often, recruiters are only thinking about how to recruit the person. Instead of seeking first to understand, they just speak to be understood. They talk and talk and tell all sorts of awesome things about their program, and the recruit is not even listening. I just think recruiters often miss this simple human relation step."

"First thing, build a relationship of trust with the recruit. Start diving in and asking what they are looking for. Ideally, what's the perfect scenario for

them? Then go into specifics of how we can help
them and how our company fits into their plan.
Connect their goals to the company and show what
kind of positive impact we can make on their
financial future."

"Ask them why they're meeting with you. Ask them
what they'd like to get out of the meeting. Let them
talk. Then listen, listen, listen."

"I want to know them. So, I ask them questions to find
out who they are, what their five-year plan is, and
where the pain is at. You've got to find the pain for
them. What is it about their current situation in their
life that's not getting them what they want? Maybe
it's renting or debt, they have no schooling, not
making ends meet, not progressing monetarily or
skill-set-wise. Once you understand their pain, only
then can you customize your opportunity to them."

During all my interviews with different recruiters,
there were only two ideas that were independently
talked about by everyone. This was one of them. A
common misconception about recruiting is that there
is a magic presentation that will close anyone. There

is no canned recruiting pitch. Every person is different. Their circumstances are different, their needs are different, their motives are different. Therefore, your presentation must be different. There is no single factor more important in the recruiting process than influence. And influence only grows as your relationship with the recruit grows. You must seek to build a relationship by genuinely getting to know them before making any attempt to recruit them.

One important side note on this subject. If your recruit has a spouse or significant other, get to know them too!

"It's super vital and key to get the spouse involved early in the process and get them around the culture."

One time I landed a recruiting meeting with a top-performing door knocker. This rep had met with multiple companies, and no one had succeeded in pulling him away from his current company. He and his wife had both been selling door-to-door for a competitor, and he was taking point on figuring out what company they were going to sell for next.

Before the meeting, I insisted that he bring his wife along as well. During the meeting, he played hard ball, asked tough questions, and leveraged other offers. As we talked, I made sure that every qualifying and get-to-know-you question I asked him, I also asked her. I facilitated the conversation in such a way that she spent an equal amount of time as him communicating her concerns, questions, and goals.

Eventually, he left the room to use the bathroom. After he walked out, his wife leaned over and said to me, "I don't care what my husband does, I'm signing with you!" When he walked back into the room, I half-joking-half-seriously informed him that his wife was coming with us, and that if he wanted to see her at all during the summer, he had no choice but to sign with us too! The rest of the meeting consisted of his wife and I ganging up on him until he agreed to sign. I'm confident that had I only met with him without having his wife there, I would not have signed them. Or at least it would have been a long, drawn-out back-and-forth discussion over several months.

Why was I so successful where so many other recruiters had failed. The reason was that I was the first recruiter to include his wife. All the other recruiters just met with him, and then he played middleman, relaying the information mixed with his opinions to her. This was the first time that she got to be an active participant in the process. Moral of the story, always include the spouse or significant other in the recruiting process!

"I love having their spouse involved. If I know they're married, I have to have their spouse if I'm going to recruit them. Repeat, if they're married, get the spouse involved. That's my go-to strategy every single time."

Now that you understand the recruit deep enough to know his or her needs and how working with you meets those needs, it's time to start painting the picture of the opportunity.

Presenting Practice Number 2
The Opportunity: Talk Long Term, Talk Big Picture

In the early 1900s, psychologists typically believed that people were primarily motivated by basic needs such as food, shelter, and clothing. 1943, Abraham Maslow published "A Theory of Human Motivation," and suggested that there were other motivational factors that humans prized even higher than the basic necessities of life. The highest of these factors, he claimed, was the pursuit of self-actualization or achieving one's full potential.

If you want your prospects to feel strongly motivated to work with you, avoid talking about how your opportunity fulfills their lowest and shortest-term needs (like money) and focus instead on how it fulfills their greatest long-term need. Show them how your opportunity will help them become the best person they can be.

"It's not just about the money, it's what the recruit

can become through the process of working with you and the company. I never, ever, ever talk money when I'm recruiting. It's all about the opportunity, what they can become, and the vision of the company. I rarely ever will talk about the pay-scale. If they ask for it I'll tell them I'll email it to them and they can contact me if they have any questions. So many recruiters just focus on the money, and the problem is that every other company is going to talk about the money in their recruiting. So, I like to focus on what everybody else isn't going to focus on, which is the program, the systems, what the rep will become through the experience and the long-term opportunity."

Personal development comes through years of mentorship, which is why the best recruiters present the job as a multi-year career rather than a short-term summer job. Even if a recruit signs easily, take the time to plant the seeds of long-term opportunity in their mind.

"I see recruiters make the same mistake over and over again. A potential recruit says he or she wants to sell, the manager gets stoked, signs them up, and

just leaves it at that. Instead, that manager should really take the time and help that new recruit truly understand what the job could be for them if they really applied themselves over the next few years. I really don't like recruiting people to come work for a season. The amount of time and energy that goes into taking someone from rookie to getting them though their first year is just so intense. I'm much more interested in a recruit who's looking for a 'mini-career.' Someone looking to do it for three to five years. It's worth your energy to spend more time on the front end painting the long-term picture and getting recruits to see it as more than just a temporary job."

Do yourself a favor and start the recruiting relationship in a way that will pay you dividends for years instead of months by presenting the long-term perspective from the start. Additionally, by infusing "long-term" into your presentation, you will attract individuals who statistically perform better.

"Research shows that a person's tendency to have a long-term perspective is the number one factor determining their success in life. So, when I meet

with a recruit, I ask about their five-year plan because I want to make sure I'm working with someone that has long-term goals."

When meeting with recruits, it's critical that you help them understand just how big and life-changing your opportunity truly is.

"Give them perspective on what the job entails entirely, not just the money. Explain all the other incredible things that come from the process. Help them have a bigger vision of what the opportunity is and how each step that they take with you is preparing them for greater opportunities down the road. Let them know that you are committed to your relationship for the long term. That you want to build and grow with them for the next three to five years."

Make sure to put the job in the context of this bigger opportunity.

"I promise everybody that works for me that I will give them at least as good of an opportunity, if not a better opportunity, than the one I had."

Most importantly, remember to apply these truths to yourself. Having a long-term perspective also means that you, as a recruiter, recognize that it can take a long time to recruit someone and become massively successful at recruiting. Recruiting is a relationship game and you can't force or rush the process.

"I've noticed that recruiters will burn the bridge too early— some people take four or five years to recruit. For example, think about the single guy that says he'll never do the job, then all of a sudden he gets married. His wife is not going to live off bread and water and sleep on the floor, so they call you up. As a recruiter, you need to be patient. The best recruiters have a long-term vision."

To summarize, as you are recruiting, interviewing, and presenting, remember the following.

First, it's not about the money, it's about the opportunity. Money is just a byproduct of becoming the best person you can be. Make sure that your recruit understands the bigger picture.

Second, it's not worth your time to recruit someone to work a summer or sometimes even one year. Recruit them to a career even if it's just a 3-5 year "mini" career.

Third, never burn a bridge; always keep positive relationships open because you never know when circumstances will place an individual back on your doorstep.

At this point in the recruiting process, you know the recruit's needs, and you know that you must instill a long-term perspective and understanding of the opportunity. But what is the best way to communicate all of this information? How can you transfer this knowledge in a way that not only makes sense but stokes emotions that gets your recruit to sign? By far, the most effective way to connect the dots and influence someone in recruiting is through stories.

Presenting Practice Number 3
Become a Master Story Teller

What if you could walk into your local thrift shop, purchase $130 of junk, and sell it online for $3,600? This is exactly what two Ph.D. researchers did.

For their study, they purchased about one hundred different worthless knickknacks. Things like paperweights, plastic fruit, old Christmas ornaments, staplers, a tiny brass boot, and a miniature coconut with a face painted on it. Each of these items cost a couple of dollars. The researchers then listed them on eBay and sold them at a 2800% profit! How were these scholars able to increase the perceived value of each of these items so much? Stories.

The listing for each item did not contain any description or details of the item. Instead, it contained a fictional short story written by a volunteer professional writer or author. One story regaled the adventures of a broken metal kangaroo-looking mouse toy named Kangamouse. Another about all the extravagant parties that a particular rusted meat thermometer got to help throw. Whatever the theme or style, every object received its own story. And these stories increased the perceived value of these objects by 280 times!

As you read the following quotes, think about how you feel when you hear a great story. This will help you understand just how powerful storytelling is in the recruiting process.

"If you wish to influence an individual, tell them a compelling story." -Annette Simmons

"Stories are powerful because they transport us into other people's worlds." -Paul Zak

"A story is a way to say something that can't be said any other way." -Flannery O'Connor

"If you're going to have a story, have a big story, or none at all." -Joseph Campbell

"All human beings have an innate need to hear and tell stories and to have a story to live by." -Harvey Cox

"Stories are the single most powerful weapon in a leader's arsenal." —Howard Gardner, Harvard University

"Many people don't realize the extent to which stories influence our behavior and even shape our culture." -Lawrence Shapiro

"A story can go where facts and analysis is denied admission: our hearts. Facts can persuade people, but it doesn't inspire them to act. To do that, you need to tell a story that fires the imagination and stirs the soul." -Harrison Monarth

Stories are powerful because they explain, illustrate, relieve recruiting pressure, build credibility, and stir emotions, all while building a relationship of trust and connection. To illustrate, I'll share a personal story about how sales changed my life.

At the age of twenty-one, I found myself pretty behind in life. A solid decade of goofing off had left with me a 1.6 high school GPA, no SAT or ACT scores, virtually no work experience, and no confidence that I could attain any level of success in my life. I had just arrived in a new state, with no friends and no work. But I knew that I didn't want to be a bum. I wanted to be successful, I just didn't know how. Until I interviewed for my first sales job. What drew me to door-to-door sales was that nobody seemed to care about my past. The door-to-door sales industry didn't care that I grew up poor, that I had been homeless, and I technically didn't graduate high school. It didn't care that I had no car or that I had been selling my plasma to pay rent! It didn't care that I was an oddball and a little weird. Sales only cared about one thing. How hard I was willing to work. I couldn't change my past, and there were so many things in my life that were out of my control, but my work ethic was not one of them. That was something I completely controlled. So I got to work.

I set a goal to outwork everyone around me every day, and I did. Over time my paychecks grew, and so did my confidence. I became a top performer and a positive influence on the people around me. I made six figures as a college freshman. I began investing in a real estate. I traveled the world. I started a family and was able to provide an incredible life for my wife and five kids. Sales changed my life by allowing me to level the playing field for myself and not only catch up but get so far ahead that I sometimes can't believe my life is even real.

If I were recruiting someone that felt like they needed an opportunity in life to catch up or get ahead, it would be impossible for that story not to resonate with them. Stories are powerful because they transport people into your world. Recruits will automatically put themselves into the story that you're sharing and apply it to their lives. It's not enough that your potential recruit understands logically why they should join you. They must feel moved to take action. And that's what using stories in your recruiting presentation will do. Take time to think through the themes and stories that will resonate with the people you meet. Is your potential recruit an underdog, trying to tackle impossibly large goals? What story could you share about someone on your team that you helped conquer some Goliath in their life? Is your potential recruit looking to grow personally into a leader? What story could you share about someone in your company that was able to go from being a low-producing rep to a powerful leader?

"If stories come to you, care for them. And learn to give them away where they are needed. Sometimes a person needs a story more than food to stay alive."
-Barry Lopez

Like arrows in a quiver, professional recruiters collect stories. Think about all the different types of people, situations, and concerns you run into in recruiting and arm yourself with stories for each of them.

"Tell the story of your company. Help them understand the vision. Show them where you've been, what you've been through, and the amazing things you are doing right now. Tell the story of where you are going, and let them know, with sincerity, that we want them to be a part of that. I've found when I do it this way, recruits will feel what I feel about this opportunity. I don't just want them to hear it, I want them to feel it."

Stories help potential recruits to relate. Stories allow them to visualize themselves being successful on your team or at your company. Consider how stories affected this recruiter's decision to get into sales.

"The guy that got me in was probably one of the best recruiters I originally saw. He related to me: I was from a small town, he was from a small town. His story of how he got to where he was resonated with me. His story hammered on hard work, which was something he knew I valued and wasn't afraid of. I had a hard time imagining myself being the type of person that would do really well at this job. But when I met my recruiter, he related to me and his story convinced me I could succeed at selling. So first, before anything else, you have to have a story. What's the story that you're going to tell when you sit down with a recruit? I'll give you some ideas. Tell the story of who we are as a company and who you are as a person. Tell the story of what got you in to this job. Be genuine, be authentic, be vulnerable. God made you who you are for a reason, so be that person— don't try to be somebody that you're not. Tell it the way it is and tell it the way you are. Don't be afraid

to tell your actual humble story. Be yourself because people are going to relate with who you are more than with who you think you should be."

Be practiced and organized in your storytelling. Top recruiters have a set format they follow and even utilize presentation decks to keep themselves on track to clearly illustrate their points. Consider crafting a story that follows the format used by this recruiter.

"When telling our story, I start with the industry and what makes our industry special compared to our entire economy. Then I go down to what makes our company special in our industry compared to the other companies. And then, I go into what makes my group special, compared to the other teams within the company. I funnel it down to the fact that this is an extremely special opportunity for them."

If you invested the time getting to know the prospective recruit (See Chapter 3: Qualifying), you will be able to use all of that information to home in on the stories that will be the most impactful to them. You will be able to use stories to frame your opportunity within the context of their life so that it's clear to them that this indeed is a very special opportunity that perfectly fits their needs.

If you want the recruit to feel the passion behind your words, tell stories. If you want them to internalize the vision of your company and truly understand how your opportunity can benefit them, tell stories. If you want them to connect with you as a person instead of seeing you as just a recruiter trying to sell them, tell stories.

These are the exact presentation techniques that the industry's top recruiters have employed to rise to seven-figure incomes. If you want to be the best, do what the best do. These practices alone should be sufficient to move a recruit through the process to commitment. Frequently, however, objections or concerns arise and a little extra know-how and effort is required to bring them to a decision. In the next chapter, you will learn seven closes that will allow you to ensure you sign the recruit every time!

1. Seek first to understand
2. Build a relationship of trust

INDUSTRY COMPANY PROGRAM

"This is a very special opportunity specifically matched to you."

Chapter Four
PRESENTING
Summary & Action Items

- Get to know the rep deeply before you talk about anything else. Remember, influence grows naturally out of relationships built on trust.

- Think and communicate in long-term and big-picture language.

- Use stories to elicit emotion and deeper connection.

Recommended Reading

- The 7 Habits of Highly Effective People by Dr. Stephen R. Covey
- Habit 4: Think Win-Win
- Habit 5: Seek first to understand, then to be understood.
- The Speed of Trust by Stephen M. Covey

- How to Win Friends and Influence People by Dale Carnegie

Write down and memorize seven questions to ask in your next recruiting meeting that will help you get to know the recruit better.

1.

2.

3.

4.

5.

6.

7.

At the beginning of the meeting, ask how much time they have and spend at least 50% of that time just getting to know them.

Make a commitment to not talk about money at all in your next recruiting interview.

Begin collecting stories—your story, other people's stories on your team or in your division, your company's origin story—and practice telling them.

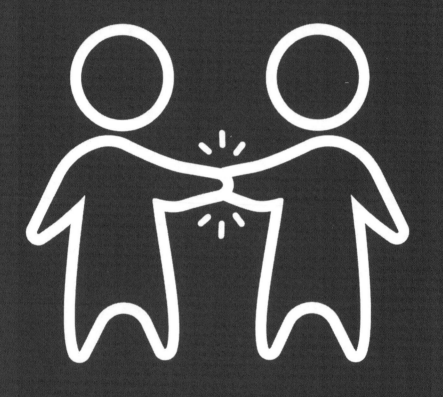

Chapter Five

OVERCOMING OBJECTIONS & CLOSING

How do I move people to decision and action?

The following closes are effective because they cause your recruit to divulge their real concerns, sell themselves on the job, truly consider the opportunity from a long-term perspective, see the simplicity in the decision, see all the value the job can provide, and make a final and committed decision to work with you!

Close Number 1
The Investor Close

This closing strategy is useful in situations where a potential recruit has decided to do door-to-door sales but is trying to decide between companies. Ask them the following question:

"If you had $100k to invest, would you invest it in our company or with [the other company]? If you wouldn't invest your money with [the other company], why would you invest a resources that's way more valuable, your time?"

If you conducted the presentation according to the practices outlined in the previous chapter, then you'll already know what the answer to this question will be. This question reframes the decision into a choice about where they're going to invest their most precious resource—their time. If they wouldn't invest their money in the other company, why would they give them their time? Follow up by asking them why they would invest their money with your company. Answers might include things like, "The other company is big but hasn't grown in years. It seems like I could grow more here." Or "You guys are more established and much safer than a sales startup." The answers they give will be their most convincing arguments for working with you. Just validate their answer and tell a story related to their answer.

Close Number 2
The Resume Close

The resume close is effective when a recruit is having a hard time looking past short-term factors like pay and seeing the long-term merits of your opportunity.

"All things equal, which company would you rather have on your resume?'"

This question is amazing because it pushes the recruit to take a long-term perspective when evaluating the decision to work with you. Maybe right now they are considering taking an odd job unrelated to their future goals because it pays a higher wage. They may not be thinking about how your opportunity will further them in their long-term career and life goals. When they respond that they would prefer to have your company on their resume, ask why. They may respond with things like "I'm trying to own my own business someday, and I know I need sales experience," or "I'm going to be applying for an MBA, and I need to show leadership experience." Their answers will be all the proof they need that working with you is what's best for their long-term interests.

Pro tip: Customize this question based on the information you gained during the presentation. For example: "When you submit your Harvard application in three years, which company would you rather have on there?" Or "When you make the transition into the finance industry, which job is going to better show you know how to work with clients?"

Close Number 3
The Sell–Me Close

This close is very effective for a recruit that is familiar with your company's success or might know people that like working there.

"Why do you think so many people consider this a good opportunity and wind up working here?"

Here's one recruiter's explanation of why he loves this close.

"This question basically asks them to sell me on the opportunity. They'll say things like, 'Well, my friends that have done this have made great money, and it's given them a lot of freedom.' Then you just agree with them. 'That's actually why most of us are here.' I always like a recruit to spell out to me why they're thinking about doing the job. Have them explain to you how the company can help them with their goals. Put them in a position where they're selling themselves on the idea rather than you trying to talk them into it."

Close Number 4
The If—Then Close

Use this close whenever a potential recruit has concerns or needs that must be met before they'll sign.

"If we could do this, this, and that, would you see any reason why you wouldn't join us?"

The 'this, this, and that' might be prerequisite needs such as: shadowing you to see the sales process; talking to other people who have worked for you; meeting a regional, VP, or owner; seeing 1099's to prove earnings; doing a dinner to let spouses meet, or any number of other things. After identifying all needs and concerns, this question is powerful because it asks the recruit to agree that they'll commit if those specific needs are met.

Once they reply affirmatively, simply take care of the needs and sign them. (You will recognize this as the concern resolution model from selling. Remember, if you know how to sell, you know how to recruit!)

Here's another version of this close:

"What does this have to look like for you in order to make sense?"

Again, you are bringing the decision to a head and asking them to act. As a recruiter, it is your responsibility to help every interested prospect make a decision. This close makes that decision very simple and easy.

Close Number 5
The Opportunity Close

Use this close when a recruiting battle has pushed the recruit to only focus on the money.

"Outside of the money, what else are you looking to gain from this opportunity?"

When multiple companies compete for a recruit, the conversation often shifts away from the value the companies can provide toward the deals they will offer. Prospective recruits become short-sighted in their thinking and stop giving proper weight to the non-monetary factors of the decision. One recruiter explains.

"I like to get their mind going in a different direction from the money. I want them to see that this opportunity will provide them so much more than just cash."

This close is effective because as previously explained, money is not a powerful enough motivator anyway. And even if it is, you want recruits to work with you for the right reasons. This close works because it asks recruits to highlight, from their perspective, what value your opportunity offers them. Once they answer this question, all that's necessary to close is to agree with them and then tell stories illustrating how others have gained what the recruit hopes to gain from your opportunity. For example, maybe a recruit wants the experience of cold calling to prepare them to run their own landscaping business. Share the story of someone that worked at your company and used the experience to later start and run their own successful business.

Close Number 6
The Worst Case Scenario Close

Use this close to make the decision safe by establishing that even in a worst-case scenario, the decision still makes sense.

"What do you need to take home this year to make it worth your time?"

With due weight given to the non-financial opportunities of the job, at the end of the day, money is still a major factor in the decision-making process. This close is very effective for two reasons. First, it gives you a clear idea of their expectations and needs. Second, it creates criteria upon which they can make a decision. This close pairs perfectly with the If-Then Close. For example, follow up this close by asking, "If you felt like it was realistic for you to earn x dollars this year, would you see any reason why you wouldn't join?" Once you and the recruit agree, show them what it will take to make that amount and how many others on your team have earned that. Use pay stubs and tell them stories as further evidence of what they can accomplish.

This close also works well with Close Number 7 below.

Close Number 7
The Safe & Simple Close

This close is successful when the prospective recruit has doubts that cause them to perceive the risk as too high or to question their ability to succeed at the job.

"If you knew this was a safe decision and that you would do well at the job, is there anything that would keep you from doing it?"

The feeling of risk or of having to make an important decision can often feel uncomfortable. Making the decision feel safe for your recruit will ease their discomfort and encourage them to join.

"There's a lesson in recruiting that I learned selling door-to-door. You have to make the decision safe. This question is a direct adaptation of the close I used when knocking. I'd ask the customer, 'If you knew this was a safe decision and that the product was going to work the way I've explained it, what would keep you from doing this?' Phrased that way, the answer is usually, 'nothing.' It's the exact same thing in recruiting. We're just too impatient; we're not

willing to recruit people the right way. The right way is not recruiting them with money. The right way is just to make the decision super safe and super simple for them. Once the recruit agrees that they would commit if they knew the decision was safe, then you just make it safe for them. How do you do that? You take them and show them. You let them shadow you. You recruit with a 'come and see', 'come and do' attitude. If you make it this simple and safe, there's absolutely no reason someone won't sign."

To iterate, if you really want to effectively close recruits, don't just tell them, show them.

"Be willing to go knock a door with someone. You'll win recruits much easier if instead of saying, 'We could go knock' you're saying, 'I'm going out on Saturday, let me show you how this is done.' That leadership of 'let me show' vs 'let me tell you' is just so powerful. It's the difference between winning and losing recruiting battles."

Remember, if you find yourself at a standstill in the recruiting process, it may be time for action!

"If you can't close a recruit by meeting, then it's time to take them knocking. Let them see a sale. If you show them the job, they will always get excited about the opportunity."

Talk is cheap, and action speaks much louder than words.

"Recruiters make the mistake of thinking they're going to sit down with a recruit and just woo him or her with their words. It takes more than that. It's amazing what happens when you get out there with a recruit and knock. The best recruiters develop a 'let me prove it' culture and lead from the front. This type of attitude and action convinces people really quick."

As a recruiter, it's important to always remember how scary the transition to commission-only sales can be. For recruits it can often feel like they are taking a major risk. The best recruiters are empathetic to this and willing to put in whatever work is necessary to prove that the decision to work with you is a safe one.

"Recruiters are unwilling to do the work, meaning

they're not willing to go out and knock with someone. You have to look at it from the recruit's shoes. You're asking them to give up their job and come work full commission. Even if they're only making ends meet at their current job, you still owe it to them to make sure this decision is safe and too many recruiters are unwilling to do that. We're unwilling to put the remote down. Unwilling to skip Monday night football or whatever it is to go knock when a recruit can knock. You'd be surprised at the power knocking with someone has to seal the deal."

Whatever opportunity or job you do, in order to win a recruit, it may be necessary to stop talking and start walking! Show them the value you can create for them and give them a taste of what it's like to work with you.

Chapter Five

OVERCOMING OBJECTIONS & CLOSING

Summary & Action Items

Memorize and master these closes. Repeat them out loud until they're rote, and like all Seven-Figure recruiters, you'll find yourself using proper and positive influence to move people toward solid commitment.

Midpoint Reflection

This is a good place to take a breather. Flip back over the pages to review what you've just consumed. Contemplate how you will apply these principles to your particular recruiting efforts. Write down two or three specific actions you will take and how those changes will affect your recruiting results. Find motivation in the fact that you are now in possession of the critical practices that have led countless other recruiters to million-dollar incomes. Once you've taken sufficient time to ensure that your learning will be applied, feel free to continue.

Chapter Six
GROWING

Create An Eternal Chain of Value, Influence, and Income

In order to earn millions of dollars of income, you need to create millions, tens of millions, or even hundreds of millions of dollars of value. It's impossible to achieve this by yourself in a short amount of time because there are only so many hours in a day and your personal sales capacity is limited. No matter how incredible of a salesperson you are, there are limits to how many accounts you can personally sell in a month, quarter, summer, or year. Therefore, you must leverage the passion and work of other people to create value through them. In this way, you can expand your value, influence, and income infinitely. This chapter will teach you exactly how to do that.

First, we will define leadership and learn how to measure your leadership depth and breadth.

Second, we will discuss the Three Levels of Influence, which are: Personal Success, Leadership, and Leading Leaders.

Third, we will deep dive into the Four Laws of Growth, which are: Commit Long Term, Prioritize Growth, Put People First, and Stay Revved.

And lastly, you'll learn a framework for identifying why people get stuck in their leadership progression and how to get unstuck!

What Is Leadership?

A few years back, a sales company contacted me and asked me to consult for them. I attended their meetings, delivered training, and spent time with their reps and the sales managers. In time I discovered a key problem in the structure of one of their offices. While the sales manager held the title and authority for the team, he did not hold the respect or the influence of the team. Through his own laziness, inconsistency, lack of personal production, and tendency to prioritize his own concerns over that of his reps, he had lost the respect of those he had formal stewardship over.

There was a person in the office that did have the respect of the team. Surprisingly, it was a rookie sales rep. This rookie sales rep had more influence over the office than the actual manager.

This rookie was hands down the hardest worker on the team. His peers saw how often he stayed out knocking past dark to hit his goals. This rep performed. Even though he was a rookie, he often outperformed the veteran reps on the team. This rep was positive. Everyone felt more optimistic and confident around him because he did his best to spread positivity everywhere he went. He genuinely and authentically cared about the team. He didn't make money on anyone in the office, but if he ever had an opportunity to create value or help someone else, he took it.

His actions and attitude organically and positively affected the thoughts, emotions, and behaviors of those around him. It was obvious to me that if the reps in the office were ever forced to choose who to follow, they would not follow the man with the title, they would follow the man with the influence. The former may have been their manager, but the latter was their leader.

From this story, we learn the definition of leadership. Leadership is human influence, nothing more, nothing less. Leadership happens when people voluntarily adjust their thoughts, emotions, and behaviors to be in harmony with your influence. This is a profound realization! It means that anyone can be a leader. You may not hold a title, but you can absolutely lead everyone around you, including those above you! Now that you understand what leadership is let's learn how to measure it.

Measuring Leadership
The Leadership Matrix

Everyone has influence, but that influence varies. Leadership influence can be quantified by its breadth and depth. Breadth is measured by the number of people you influence. Do you consistently affect the thoughts, feelings, and behavior of only one other person or thousands of people?

Depth is measured by how impactful that influence is. Is your influence barely surface level, affecting people in only the smallest ways? Or is it deep and profound, shaping and changing the trajectory of their lives? Is your influence recognizable to people? Do they see your influence as a source of value in their life? Do they believe that they will become better people under your influence? Do they desire more of your influence in their life?

Some individuals, like Gandhi, Buddha, Jesus, and even businesspeople like Steve Jobs, deeply influence the entire world. Their influence is wide and deep and continues to operate even after their deaths. Their influence transcends time and barriers. You can become like them. Through the influence you wield, you can also become immortal and create value that is exponentially greater than what you could ever individually produce. In order to maximize your influence, and by extension your income, you need to deeply impact as many people as you possibly can. By pairing proper positive influence with the recruiting techniques taught in this book, you will unlock the door to unlimited income. Seven figures will just be the beginning.

Let's discuss these two measures of influence in greater detail.

Depth

Influence is the effect that one person has on another person's thoughts, feelings or behaviors. But this effect can vary in degree. Shallow influence means that the effect you have on another person's thoughts, feelings, or behavior is mild. Deep influence means that the effect is profound. If you have shallow influence over a rep, maybe you periodically give them something interesting to think about. Or maybe they like being around you because you're fun. Contrast this to having influence so deep that you change someone's entire life for the better. Or being their primary source of inspiration or motivation in their life.

The first thing you should focus on as a leader is deepening your influence with your people. How can you be a bigger positive influence in their life? How can you become more valuable and relevant to them? How can you better exemplify their ideal self? How can you help them win and achieve their dreams?

The simplest and most impactful way to deepen your influence with another person is to spend time with them. A personal story illustrates this.

Sam had a less-than-ideal upbringing. Turmoil at home led him to a troubled lifestyle. At a young age, Sam found himself on a path that did not lead to his ideal self. When I started working with Sam, he didn't love work. He was pretty lazy and was content just scraping by and having a good time. As I got to know Sam, however, it became obvious to me that he wanted more for his life. He wanted success, he wanted confidence, and he wanted to be a force for good in the world, but fear, insecurities, and bad habits were holding him back. So I invested into Sam. I spent time with him. Sam loved fishing, and so we fished. Just he and I, hanging out, talking, getting to know each other. Sam looked up to me and knew I was extremely busy, so it was really meaningful to him that I made time for him. As our relationship grew, I communicated to Sam that I saw potential in him. I nurtured the ambitions that I knew he had inside. I told him I believed he could be a top performer and an amazing leader. He could be someone that others looked up to and followed.

Because of our relationship and the respect he had for me, he believed me. He began to see himself the way that I saw him. He internalized the vision of this better life and really started to believe that he could create it. This changed everything for Sam. He immediately started outworking everybody on the team. As a result, he outperformed them. He climbed the ranks. He called up every single person he knew and tried to recruit them to come sell with him. One night I was lying in bed about to fall asleep when I received a text from Sam. The picture was of him and seven recruits inside of a customer's home holding up an iPad with a digitally signed contract. Everyone, including the customer, was smiling. All on his own, Sam had rounded up buddies to go on an impromptu out-of-state sales trip. I hadn't asked or even prompted him, he just did it. Fueled by his newfound passion for success, he started dominating.

Sam was now a different person. The trajectory of his life was pointed in a better direction. His confidence, happiness, and positive influence increased. He saw in his mind's eye a vision of how incredible his future could be. He saw that he was more than his old habits and that he could grow to become whoever he wanted. I was so happy for Sam. I felt incredible joy from being a part of Sam's journey, and I looked forward to being able to watch him grow and progress as a person. This happiness, however, would not last. While knocking one day, I received a text from one of my other reps.

"Sam is dead."
My brain saw the words but refused to accept the possibility of their truth. It was like a strange disconnect between understanding logically what something meant and not being able to comprehend it. I texted back. "What do you mean?" I received a reply. "Sam is dead. He's gone. His brother found him in his room this morning, and he had passed away in the night."

I immediately called the rep that was texting me and was told the same thing. By the end of the conversation, my brain had accepted the reality of what had happened. I hung up, gripped the steering wheel of my car like a vice grip and screamed. Then began sobbing and hyperventilating uncontrollably. Sam was gone. His path had ended.

Sam's death would've been tragic, even if he hadn't started making monumental positive changes in his life. It also would've been tragic if he had spent decades progressing, achieved his goals, and then passed. But the fact that he passed so quickly after seeing and understanding his true potential still upsets me. Sometimes I feel angry that he was only able to experience the joy of success for such a short period of time, but other times I feel grateful that he was able to see it and taste it before he left this Earth. And I especially feel grateful that I was able to be a part of that experience for Sam, however small my role may have been. I think that if at the end of my life I were required to give an accounting of the good I did on Earth, I would definitely point to the work I did with Sam. There were many people in his life that contributed to his transformation but knowing that I had a part means everything to me. That time I spent with him feels more meaningful and important than all the accounts I personally sold combined. The depth of influence that I was able to have on one person and the effect that it had on their life changed my life. A poem I read recently perfectly characterizes the experience for me.

"If you help others with all your might
to achieve the goals within their sight
the strength you derive from their delight
will pull you up to greater heights."
-Roy Lee Barrett

Ask yourself:

Who in your circle of influence do you need to spend more time with?

What personal development needs to happen in your life in order for you to become the type of person that others look up to?

How will deepening your positive influence on others enrich your own life?

How can you deepen your influence on the people in your life?

Breadth

Influence is defined as the effect that one person has on another person's thoughts, feelings or behaviors. We just learned that you should do everything you can to deepen that effect, but if you want to maximize your influence, you also need to consider how many people you influence.

Influence breadth is measured by the quantity of people that you influence. In order to achieve a Seven-Figure Summer, you need to not only deepen your influence, but widen it. Make it your goal to positively influence as many people as you possibly can. Rastafarin musician Bob Marley used his music to positively influence millions of people. To share his quote again, "The greatness of a man is not in how much wealth he acquires, but in his integrity and his ability to affect those around him positively."

It should be your goal to positively affect as many people as you possibly can. This influence can happen in person as you interact with others one-on-one. It can happen through content you create and distribute online or by writing a book for someone to read! It can also happen through other people, as you'll learn about in the upcoming section, "The Three Levels of Influence."

Now that you understand influence depth and breadth, we can calculate your leadership score. Ask yourself, on a scale from 1-10, 1 being super shallow and 10 being profoundly deep, how you would rate the depth of influence you have with other people? Now ask yourself, on a scale from 1-10, 1 being hardly anybody and 10 being nearly everybody, how would you rate the breadth of your influence?

Let's compare influence to water. Imagine that everyone in your city is dying of thirst, and you are the only one that has any water. They all need their jugs filled, and only you can do it! You have to choose how to deliver the water, either through a straw, a hose, a sprinkler, or a massive raincloud downpour. In picking the best option, you need to think about how much water you can push out and to how many people.

Depth of Influence

	Shallow	Deep
Many	Sprinkler	Downpour
Few	Straw	Hose

Breadth of Influence

A straw would obviously be the worst. You'd only be able to deliver a tiny stream of water to one person at a time. A hose would be better because you could pump out much more water than a straw, but you'd still be very limited to how many people you could serve. With a sprinkler, you could spray lots of people at once, but they each would only get a little bit of water. But imagine a massive downpour that spans your entire city. That downpour could deliver millions of gallons of water to every single person in the city all at once!

When it comes to your influence, what are you? Are you a straw, influencing very few people in a very small way? Are you a hose, providing lots of influence, but only to a small number of people? Are you a sprinkler, influencing lots of people in a very small way? Or are you a downpour, influencing everyone in a deep and meaningful way.

Take a look at the leadership matrix and see which quadrant you fall into. By working to increase the depth and breadth of your influence, you will begin to maximize your potential as a leader, increase your positive impact on the world, and significantly grow your income.

Now that you understand leadership, let's talk about the three levels of leadership that you will progress through as you expand the depth and breadth of your influence.

The 3 Levels of Leadership

Level 1: Personal Success (Sales Rep)

Remember that titles do not grant you influence, just authority. You can use your formal position to command and control, but not to capture hearts and minds. You access these only through proper positive influence.

Someone else with a title can bestow you a title of your own, but they can't force people to follow you. So how do get followers? By becoming someone that people want to follow. Are you a person that others would want to emulate? Do they wish they could be

The 3 Levels of Leadership

Level 3
Leading Leaders

Level 2
Leadership

Level 1
Personal Success

like you, in general or in some specific area? Would
they trade places with you if they could in that area?
Do you represent the future attainment of their goals?
Does deepening their relationship with you help them
feel closer to their ideal self? By achieving massive
success in your life and maximizing your human
potential, in time you will become a person that
others naturally want to follow. There is no shortcut
to authentic leadership. No amount of puffed-up
accolades or social media titles will get you there.
You must become the type of person that others want
to follow. Efforts to lead must constantly be mirrored
by efforts to become the best person you can be.
Either generally or specifically in the area in which
you want to be influential. A story illustrates this
idea.

There was once a rep that I really wanted to recruit.
We only knew each other casually, but I knew
enough about him to know that I wanted to work
with him. And he knew enough about me that he
believed I could help him reach his goals. He had
watched me work, lead, and succeed for years. He
looked up to me in all of these things and wanted to
duplicate that success for himself. In short, he wanted

to be influenced by me, at least in the professional dimension of his life.

And so when I made the call, he responded. I explained my vision for him and what I believed he could accomplish working with me. He joined my team, and I had the positive impact on his life that he hoped for. I became his leader, not because my title outranked his in the organization, but because I influenced his thoughts, feelings, and behaviors in a deeply meaningful way that allowed him to progress professionally faster than he could on his own. I wasn't his spiritual or intellectual leader, I was his sales leader. I had earned that role through years of maximizing my own potential as a sales rep, recruiter, trainer, and manager. Interestingly though, this rep would also become my leader.

This rep had spent years invested heavily into maximizing his potential in the physical dimension of his life. He had spent a decade studying nutrition, lifting weights, and mastering a myriad of exercise programs and disciplines. Health and fitness were areas of weakness in my life but an area of strength in his. He was in better shape than me, stronger than

me, healthier than me, fitter than me, more
disciplined in the gym than me, and understood far
more about fitness than I did. So when it came to
fitness and health, I sought out his leadership and
influence. I asked if I could work out with him. He
taught me what he knew, motivated me to work out,
and positively affected my thoughts, feelings, and
behaviors in ways that made me a fitter and healthier
person. In this way, he was my leader. I led and
influenced him in his work, he led and influenced me
in the gym.

From this example, it should be clear that authentic
leadership springs naturally from becoming the best
person you can be. Think about your office, region,
or company. The top performing rep always
automatically has influence because everyone wants
to be like him or her. It doesn't matter whether or not
that individual has a formal leadership title. It doesn't
matter whether or not that individual even wants to
be a leader. Their success gives them influence
because, as a top performer, everyone on the team
wants to be more like them, at least as far as sales go.

Attempting to lead without a consistent effort to become the best person you can be in the area you want to lead is deceptive and manipulative. Don't be that person. Be a person that people actually want to follow. Maximize your human potential in all areas of your life, but specifically the areas in which you want to be a leader. Become the best sales rep, best recruiter, and best trainer, and best manager.

The first level of leadership doesn't involve anyone but yourself. Before you attempt to lead other people, you need to at least aspire to and be actively working toward achieving top 1% success in the area in which you want to lead. (For tips on how to do this, read The Six Figure Summer!) And don't worry about being perfect before you lead. Simply being on the path and consistently striving for your potential is enough to inspire and positively influence others.

Level 2: Leadership (Sales Manager)

Once you have achieved personal success or are confident in your ability to stay on the path of success, it's time to turn your attention outward and

The 3 Levels of Leadership

	Level 1	Level 2	Level 3
Level	Personal Success	Leadership	Leading Leaders
Production Source	Yourself	Your Recruits	Your Recruit's Recruits
Production Capacity / Value Creation Potential	Limited	Limited	Unlimited
Example Positions	Sales Rep	Sales Manager	Sales Regional

take on the mantle of leadership. For me, selling no longer felt that exciting after I reached my sales peak. Once I plateaued in my personal sales, I started yearning for new opportunities of growth and development. For me, that came through leadership. Recruiting, mentoring, and coaching other people to be successful was new and exciting. It gave me an opportunity to grow endlessly, to experience new challenges, and to expand my income and influence.

As you progress from level 1 to level 2 leadership, you use the influence you gained from personal success to attract and positively impact other people's lives. You widen your influence by recruiting a sales team. This is what makes door-to-door sales the greatest opportunity on the planet. It's the simplest and quickest way to change lives. There is an infinite supply of people in the world looking for a great work opportunity. They want to find a mentor to care enough about them to help them level up. Because you invested the effort into maximizing your potential, you are now in a position to maximize theirs.

One of the distinguishing factors of Leadership is that you can create value beyond your own capacity by helping your recruits and team members be more successful. For example, let's say you can sell 100 accounts in a year. If you train ten people to do the same, then you have 10x'ed your value. This is awesome, but at Level 2, you are still limited. If your influence only comes from you personally, then that influence will become more shallow as your team grows because you can only personally interact with so many people. As your sales team grows, you will want to start thinking about your transition to Level 3 leadership.

Level 3: Leading Leaders (Sales Regional)

The pinnacle of influence is Leading Leaders. This phase unlocks the portal to limitless influence, limitless production, and limitless income. You are not just teaching someone how to sell more accounts, you are teaching them how to lead other people. They can then do the same for others, and you can start a chain of leadership that perpetuates forever. You use your influence to elevate and empower, constantly seeking to bring the people around you to your current level so that you can rise even higher.

Jocko Willink, retired Navy Seal Platoon leader, said it well, "The goal of all leaders should be to work themselves out of a job. When mentored and coached properly, the junior leader can eventually replace the senior leader, allowing the senior leader to move on to the next level of leadership."

For example, suppose you teach and motivate ten of your reps to recruit and train other reps. They each then go out and recruit and train ten reps. And now you have 100 reps selling that each produce 100 accounts.

As a solitary rep, you produced 100 accounts. As a manager, you produced 1000 accounts. But as a regional/vp/divisional, you produced 10000 accounts because you produced leaders who produced leaders. In the third level of leadership, influence, production, and income is limitless because you can indirectly influence an unlimited amount of people.

There is another very important distinction with Level 3 leadership. While levels 1 and 2 can be slow and linear, level 3 is explosively fast and exponential. This is because your growth begins to compound once you start leveraging the work, talent, and passion of other people. Be patient as you grow your sales team. At first, the number of people of your team will only grow as you personally do the work of recruiting. But as you have recruits and start to empower them to recruit, manage, and lead, your organization will grow rapidly.

You should aspire to become a level 3 leader. Level 3 unlocks unlimited value, unlimited growth, and unlimited income. Leading leaders is one of the raddest experiences that life has to offer.

To summarize, your leadership journey starts with putting yourself on the path to maximizing your personal potential. It then transitions to helping other people to do the same. It finishes with producing leaders who can duplicate this entire process indefinitely.

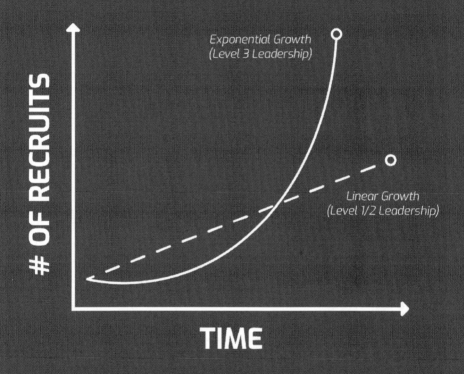

Exponential Growth
(Level 3 Leadership)

Linear Growth
(Level 1/2 Leadership)

OF RECRUITS

TIME

Unfortunately, many aspiring leaders get stuck in their journey. Let's talk candidly about why that happens. As you read, think through about situation and try to identify what has been holding you back.

Obstacles To Growth

Complacency

"Good is the enemy to great." -Jim Collins

Jim Collins conducted an academic analysis to determine what makes the all-star companies in every industry so different. He found that the single biggest inhibitor to greatness was not poor performance but good performance. Companies that were doing good became complacent and stopped striving for greatness. In the same manner, initial successes in growth can become a barrier to your future growth if you allow complacency to creep in.

People often get stuck in Level 1, (Personal Success), not because they are failing at sales, but because they are succeeding! Most reps experience several years of growth in their personal sales and income before they finally cap out. You likely will grow for many years as well which is awesome! But don't let it stop you from looking forward to the inevitable day when you will cap out in your personal production. When that happens, you will need Level 2: Leadership (Management) in order to continue progressing.

Once you get to Level 2, don't commit the same mistake! As a sales manager, there may be even more years of growth opportunities because management offers so many exciting challenges and opportunities for growth, both financially and personally. You may be able to continue growing your sales team for years before you cap out. Don't let this stop you from looking forward to the inevitable day when your team becomes so large that you plateau. When that happens, you will need to start leading leaders in order to continue progressing. You'll have to elevate your reps to replace you so you can rise to regional/vp/director. Complacency is a major reason why aspiring leaders get stuck. Don't let it happen to you! Another reason leaders get stuck is the desire for comfort.

Comfort

Growing pains hurt. It's extremely uncomfortable to put yourself in a position where you must face your inadequacies or weakness. Often people spend so much time and emotional energy maximizing their personal sales that the thought of starting at the bottom as a manager is too much to stomach. Nobody wants to be a rookie again! You spent so much time getting to a place of proficiency that you're resistant to reset and start a new learning curve.

The same comfort trap applies as you transition from Level 2 to Level 3. After several years you will hit your stride as a manager, and the last thing you'll want to do is reset, give up your power, and step into the new role of Regional/Divisional/VP.

Comfort is a major reason why aspiring leaders get stuck. Don't let the comfort zone stop you from growing. Another reason leaders get stuck is fear.

Fear

The final retardant of growth is fear and insecurity. Too many people choose not to see their potential as leaders and managers. (See Chapter Seven: The Three Deadly Sins Of Recruiting) They won't envision themselves running teams, speaking in front of groups, mentoring other people, and regionally managing. If you don't internalize the vision of how big and positive your influence can be, you will never even attempt to achieve it.

There is another way that fear prevents many sales managers from becoming regionals. In order to grow from a manager to a Regional/Division/VP, you need to push your team out from underneath you and let one of your leaders run it. Then you need to backfill and create a new team. Many managers, often without realizing it, are afraid to empower their people to replace them. They're afraid that they won't be able to repeat their success and build more teams. So instead, they keep their people down and underneath them. Do not let fear prevent you from empowering your people so that you can rise to Level 3 Leadership.

Why Getting Stuck is Such a Problem

You might reason that if you are comfortable and experiencing success, why is it necessary to grow?

Getting Stuck At Level 1: Personal Success (Sales Rep)

The problem with staying at Level 1 is that you can't grow indefinitely because your production is exclusively tied to your physical effort, which is limited. You will inevitably hit your personal production cap and sales will no longer be fun or give you the same satisfaction and meaning it used to. Additionally, because it can take a while to successfully make the transition to Managing, you will most likely find yourself in the extremely painful position of experiencing zero growth, sometimes for multiple years. You've capped out in Level 1, and you haven't yet gained growth momentum in Level 2. This is the Death Cap taught in Chapter 2, and it's scary because it can destroy your career. It's here that a lot of people quit and go looking for greener pastures.

Getting Stuck At Level 2: Leading (Sales Manager)

In order to succeed in Level 2, it's not enough that you are growing, your people have to be growing as well. If you don't help them grow, they'll leave you for someone who will help them grow.

If you stop progressing at Level 2, you will find yourself having to replace parts of your downline each year as your reps hit their personal Death Cap and fall off. If you keep your people at Level 1, they won't be your people for long. Too many managers rise to Level 2 but do not give their people the opportunity to do the same. Here's why this is such a deadly mistake:

"The best recruiters I know break their people off and rebuild their teams over and over and over again. They push their people out to run teams and then have the confidence to go rebuild a new office. The best recruiters I know make sure that their people

receive the same opportunities to lead and manage that they've received. Confidence as a manager is knowing you can go out and grind and replace a new team. I've seen it over and over again. Your whole team could die in a fiery bus crash, and the next year you just start from scratch and build a new team."

Breaking your reps off to manage is scary because it leaves you without a team. However, it's absolutely necessary in order to continue your growth. It's good for you— It puts pressure on you to keep building, and it also reassures your people that you are a successful leader because of your hustle and talent, not because you sit back and rest on the backs of your people.

The Solution to the Problem

Conscientiously install a complacency, comfort, and fear meter right on the helm of your Leader Ship. Monitor them. Once any of them get too high, course correct. Here's some tips for breaking free whenever you become trapped.

Combat Complacency

Keep yourself hungry. Commit yourself to opportunities that are currently outside of your skill set. Commit to recruiting and running a team even though you may have never done it. Commit to regionally managing even if you barely have enough reps for one office right now. Commit to making more money this year than you think is possible. Remember, he who rests, rusts!

Combat Comfort

Form a habit of actively attacking things that are outside of your comfort zone in all areas of your life. Review the promise you made at the beginning of this book and look for new opportunities to keep it.

Combat Fear

Internalize the vision of Level 3: Leading Leaders. Like an architect creating the blueprints for a mansion, you must first rise to Level 3 leadership in your mind before it will happen in reality. Make the vision of leading your internal reality and watch the universe bend itself to actualize your vision. Next you will learn the four laws of growth. These laws will allow you to quickly and consistently progress toward a massive and successful sales program.

The First Law Of Growth
Commit For The Long—Term

A setback in my recruiting career almost took me out of the game. In my eighth year in door-to-door sales, I ran a successful team in Dallas, Texas. We crushed our goals as an office, and I was a top ten rep in the company in my personal sales. We concluded the summer and headed back to Utah to start making plans for the next summer. But as the end of the year approached, nobody from the team signed up for a second summer. Not one. After eight years of work, I was back at square one. I was now just a solitary rep with no team. I contemplated giving up on my recruiting career. I had given it such a long hard effort and had nothing to show for it. After much introspection, however, I decided to give it one more shot. Getting back on the recruiting horse after taking that hard of a fall was one of the hardest things I've ever had to do. I decided if I was going to give it one last shot, I was going to give it everything I had. So I got to work. In six months, I rebuilt the team I had lost. We had a phenomenal year, and I parlayed that success into a second successful year. I split my team and grew into a regional role, doubling my production year after year after year.

In "Presenting Practice Number 2: The Opportunity: Talk Long Term, Talk Big Picture," you learned the importance of presenting sales not as a short-term job, but as a career with massive long-term opportunity. It's important to practice what you preach in recruiting! Make sure you apply this same long-term approach to yourself! The transition to becoming a professional recruiter takes time and commitment. It can be far more uncomfortable and slower than you anticipate, but you must be patient.

Personal development is a process that can't be forced. You learn and grow through experience. Developing other people's potential is messy and time-consuming work. There's no fast track. It just takes time.

Listen to how this recruiter slogged through years of recruiting effort before his growth exploded. These are fairly extreme examples of how long it may take for your sales program to take off, but it powerfully exemplifies the type of long-term commitment you must embody in order to successfully build a sales program.

"I'm the perfect example of a rep that struggled to recruit. My first year, I recruited fifteen people and only three went out. Then my second year, nobody came back, so I started over again. I brought out five new people that summer. Then the next year, only one of those reps came back. Then year four I recruited eighteen people and lost all but four. I started year five with four recruits. Going into year six, I had only five recruits. But that's the year when I finally picked up my key leaders. People think recruiting should be easy, but it takes consistent hard work. I was on campus recruiting three days a week and talking to everyone I knew for six years before I made it."

Because it can take time to gain growth traction, start now! Remember the Death Cap from Chapter 1? Even if you are making incredible money from your personal sales, if you are not recruiting and growing then you will eventually start to feel stagnant and disappointed. Plan for growth now by starting to recruit and grow early. Don't delay because you feel satisfied with the money you are making from personal sales!

Stepping onto the leadership path early is an awesome safety net against the Death Cap because even if recruiting comes slow at first, you'll be enjoying a positive growth trajectory with your personal sales. Your personal sales and income will be growing every year while you learn how to recruit and grow a team. This will keep you stoked and engaged with sales. If you wait until you max out on personal sales, you may not have a long enough runway to get through the initial few years of learning how to recruit and grow. Remember, it's not the money that keeps you stoked, it's the growth!

So start recruiting, leading, and growing before you're forced to. And remember that recruiting is a multi-year commitment. You can't assess your success as a recruiter or the viability of a recruiting career after one year or even a couple of years of effort. Check out the mindset that this recruiter persistently held year-after-year. Observe how it allowed him to stick to recruiting despite repeated failures.

"As far as recruiting goes, you may as well give it hell. You have absolutely nothing to lose. Just don't get frustrated. Even if you work hard and recruit all year and have nobody, oh well! You can still go sell a ton of accounts, make a lot of money, and try recruiting again next year."

One day my daughter wanted to grow a strawberry plant, so she buried a seed in a cup of water-soaked soil. The next morning she came into my room, completely distraught, holding the cup. There was no strawberry plant. Just dirt. In her mind, something was wrong. It seemed to her that either the seed was bad or that she wasn't taking care of it correctly. I explained to her that the plant was growing but that it was so slow she couldn't see it. Deep in the soil, the seed had already begun the spouting process, and in time would surface and then grow the fruit that she wanted.

Recruiters are often like my daughter. They shoulder tap on campus once, reach out to a couple of people online, do a few interviews, and then wonder why they don't have a massive door-to-door team. They conclude that either recruiting doesn't work or they're no good at it. So they quit and go back to their comfort zone in personal sales. This is a mistake.

Commit to recruiting and growth for the long haul, and start now. This will allow you to withstand the failures that will inevitably come as you start your growth journey.

The Second Law Of Growth
Prioritize Growth

Did you know that the average business in America is unprofitable for the first three years? Successful entrepreneurs start their businesses understanding that they will make a front-end sacrifice of time, energy, and money, to build something that pays massive long-term dividends. To use a phrase from Clayton Christensen's "Innovators Dilemma," they are patient for profit and impatient for growth. This means that great entrepreneurs prioritize growth.

Recruiting and team building is an entrepreneurial pursuit. It also requires a front end sacrifice of time, energy, and money, but pays massive long-term dividends on the back end.

If your motivation for recruiting and managing is because you need money now, don't waste your time. Stick with personal sales.

The transition from Rep to Manager and Manager to Regional can not only be extremely uncomfortable, but sometimes unprofitable in the short term. When you make the transition from sales rep to sales manager, it's very possible that the money you earn your first year managing will be less than you could've made just selling. This is because you've shifted part of your time and energy from an activity you have mastered and developed to an activity that you are learning and is in development. Aspiring door-to-door leaders trip themselves up with logic like, "When I add up the overrides I made recruiting, training, and managing this rep, it doesn't even compare to the commissions I would've made if I had spent that time selling." While that may be true, this is a scarcity mentality that will stunt your long-term growth.

Similarly, when you make the transition from sales manager to sales regional, it's very possible that the money you earn your first year regionally managing multiple teams will be less than you would've made just managing one big team. As you empower people beneath you and shift overrides from you to them, you may compare the amount of work you are putting in as a Regional to the amount of money you made and realize that you would've made more money managing one big team.

Have faith that sacrificing on the front end will translate into exponentially greater earnings in the long run. Betting on your people and investing in their growth is never a bad decision. Even if you could make more money today, this week, or this year by shirking recruiting and just selling, you are trading off infinitely larger earnings down the road for smaller returns right now. Go a little hungry right now so that you can fatten the golden goose that will produce for you forever!

Will the transition to leadership always require a financial step back? No way. Even though it's possible that recruiting will be unprofitable in the short term, for many, it actually accelerates their earnings. Having a team increases accountability and gives deeper motivation to raise the bar on your personal sales.

Listen to this recruiter's reflections on the positive impact recruiting had on his personal sales. As you read about the start of his selling career, identify the ways in which recruiting may actually increase your own personal sales and earnings.

"I really feel I could've got to divisional president a year or two quicker if I had started recruiting my rookie year. I feel I would've sold more personally because I would've felt accountable to my reps. I would've prepared more because I would've known that I needed to lead them from the front. And at the end of that first year, I would've already had my team. I didn't know any of that stuff so I went out and sold one or two summers before I even started recruiting and I'm confident I could've progressed two years quicker if I would've recruited more when I

was first starting. "

Prioritize growth. Be patient for profits that come from managing. Be prepared for it to take time. Continue to pay the bills with personal sales while you build your skillset and team. But make growth your number one priority.

The Third Law Of Growth
Take Care of Your People

The single greatest obstacle to growth is retention. The door-to-door industry is full of companies that can recruit but can't retain. As a result, they are like a car spinning its wheels. Lots of energy and activity, but no movement. You cannot build a door-to-door sales empire if you do not retain your people. Thankfully, there is an easy way to ensure your people stick around. Just take care of them. Treat them with respect, fairness, and transparency. Conversely, if you want to lose your people, don't be honest or transparent. The quickest way to lose your reps is to take advantage of them.

"You can sheer a sheep many times, but you can only skin him once. If you take care of your people, even if you only have just one or two people, they'll come back every year and they'll provide you wool for many years. If you try and take advantage of them, you'll get a benefit once and that's it."

Poor retention is a career killer for even the best recruiters. It's so much work to recruit and train sales reps that you'll burn out and quit if your people don't stay. Taking care of your people means focusing on their needs.

"Seek the benefit of your reps before your own benefit. Focus on creating opportunities for them. Focus on growth. You must constantly ponder over one question: How do I grow my people? What do they want to get out of the job, and what type of life do they hope to live? What's this job going to do for them? If you can answer these questions, then there's no limit to your success in recruiting. Live by the words of Zig Ziglar, "You can have everything in life you want if you will just help enough other people get what they want."

If you're having trouble figuring out how to create meaningful value for your people, just think about how to make their job easier for them.

"Everybody likes to find more efficient ways to get to the top. If you can figure out how to provide these 'life hacks' to your people, then you will be giving real value and your recruits will stick around."

Think about your path in the industry and see if you can make that path better for your people than it was for you.

"The best recruiters I know make sure that their people receive the same opportunities to lead and manage that they've received."

Remember that the key to unlocking seven-figure annual income in door-to-door sales is to progress from a sales rep to sales manager, to a sales regional. The only way to succeed as a sales manager is help other people become successful sales reps. And the only way to become a successful regional manager is to help other reps become successful sales managers. For a sales leader, the reps in their downline are their most important customers. You need to constantly replace yourself and help others rise to your level so that you can rise to the next.

The Fourth Law Of Growth
Stay Revved

Harry Potter stood in front of the Mirror of Erised, the last challenge to obtaining the Sorcerer's Stone. The mirror was the gateway to obtaining the stone, a magical relic that granted its possessor immortality. The evil Lord Voldemort had tried in futility to use the mirror to obtain the stone, but as Harry gazed in, the stone immediately appeared in his pocket.

Why was Harry able to receive the stone when Voldemort could not? Because the mirror was a paradox. Anyone who desired the stone for personal gain could not get it. Only one who did not wish it would receive it.

Growth is also a paradox. Like the Mirror of Erised that only grants the prize to those with correct desires, growth will only come to those who recruit with correct intentions. Those who recruit for the purpose of getting themselves off of the doors, off the phones, out of the trenches and out of the grind will never make it. If your people know you view them as your ticket to escaping the type of work you are recruiting them to do, they will not be your people for long! Without realizing it, you will emanate a stink that will repel people from working with you. The following quote came in response to the question, what's the biggest mistake recruiters make as they transition from manager to regional?

"This is so freaking easy, they quit knocking. And then they don't understand why their teams flounder. I knocked on doors hard until we were over 15,000 alarm accounts. If you are trying to become a regional so you can get off the doors, then you have an expiration date like a gallon of milk at the grocery store. You're not going to make it. It's hard to travel around and knock with reps, but that's what made my region successful. I would stay at offices for a whole week and take reps out knocking. I would take reps out with me and let them see sales every day. As a regional, even though I wasn't running a specific

team, I was on the doors every day of the summer. With reps shadowing me every single day. I wasn't knocking to try and hit a pay level. I was knocking to show reps how to sell. I was training by selling. I just see so many regionals that feel like knocking is below them. That's the biggest mistake. "

Increasing your income through recruiting is a noble endeavor. Maximizing your human potential by taking on new leadership challenges is a worthy cause. Spreading a life-changing opportunity to as many people as you can is an admirable ambition. Using people as a stepping stone to make your life easier is disrespectful and will bring you disaster. Your intentions will determine your destination before you even begin your journey.

Remember, speed of the leader, speed of the team. Lead from the front. Inspire with action and performance. A management title is not a pass to take your foot off the gas. Nothing will kill your program faster. Besides, as we learned in the First Law of Growth, "Commit For The Long Term", you likely will still need the income from your personal sales while you grow your downline. You can't afford to stop selling yet!

Memorize and live by The Four Laws of Growth, which are: Commit For The Long Term, Prioritize Growth, Put People First, and Stay Revved. By doing so you will ensure growth success. Go back to the very start of this book and read my personal growth journey. As you do, try to identify how I limited my own progression and what I could've done to accelerate my path to sales regional. Think about the ways that these four laws of growth would've accelerated my growth as a leader.

Chapter Six
GROWING
Summary & Action Items

- Leadership is the portal to immortality.

- Leadership is influence, nothing more, nothing less.

- Increase the number of people you influence, then deepen that influence.

- Progress through the three levels of leadership.

> Level 1: Personal Success (Sales Rep)
> Level 2: Leadership (Sales Manager)
> Level 3: Leading leaders (Sales Regional)

- Don't get stuck! Identify and attack complacency, comfort, and fear.

- Live by the Four Laws of Growth

    Commit for the long term.
    Prioritize growth.
    Put people first.
    Stay Revved.

Recommended Reading

- The 21 Irrefutable Laws of Leadership by John C. Maxwell
- The 15 Invaluable Laws of Growth by John C. Maxwell
- The 7 Habits of Highly Effective People by Dr. Stephen R. Covey
- Habit 2: Begin with the end in mind.
- Appendix 1, Sin #2

Chapter Seven
The Three Deadly Sins of Recruiting
Avoid These At All Costs!

Sometimes success doesn't just involve adopting correct practices, it also requires avoiding bad ones! These three "Dearly Sins of Recruiting" represent the worst and most often committed errors recruiters make. Learn them so you can avoid them!

The First Sin Of Recruiting
Limiting Yourself with Labels & Language

"You want to know the first mistake recruiters make? They label themselves as 'not the recruiter type.' If you change your language, you'll change your results."

As I reflect on over a decade of mentoring and training door-to-door recruiters, this is one of the most disheartening for me. Future sales regionals die in the womb because they refuse to see the potential they truly have as recruiters and leaders. Truly the only thing holding you back from becoming a Regional Manager, President or Billionaire CEO is your own self-perception.

"Our people just need to expand their vision of themselves and see the value they are truly capable of providing to their company and to those around them. All a recruiter needs to do is just make a decision to go recruit and manage a thousand people and they'll get there."

If you want to succeed at recruiting and building your door-to-door empire, start thinking about yourself and talking about yourself as if you have already achieved your greatest recruiting ambitions. Your thoughts and your language will create your reality, so you may as well conscientiously create the reality you want! Let the awesomeness of your opportunity fuel your recruiting confidence!

"Some people try to say recruiting is just not for them. I say that's BS. Anybody can recruit if they believe in the company they work for. I mean, come on! Do you believe in the product? Do you believe in the company? Do you believe in the vision and direction the company is going? If you answered 'yes' to those questions, you have the ability to recruit people."

Think deep and be honest with yourself: Are there self-limiting beliefs you harbor about your potential? Have you classified yourself in a way that excludes you from participating in the profoundly meaningful and rewarding work of recruiting and building sales teams? Does the language you use reflect the language of a regional, president or owner? Or is it the language of someone still trying to figure out if recruiting is "their thing?" The first step on the path toward a seven-figure recruiting income is to adjust your self-perception and your words to harmonize with your aspirations.

The Second Sin Of Recruiting
Talking Too Much In The Interview

Remember the First Rule of Presenting in Chapter 4, Build A Relationship Of Trust? This sin represents the opposite of that! I asked multiple top-tier recruiters "what are the biggest mistakes recruiters make?" Here's what they said.

"Don't let your ego get in the way. So many recruiters fall into the trap of talking. They just talk the whole meeting about themselves. The meeting becomes a measuring contest where the recruiter tries to use the potential recruit to build themselves up. The other person is not engaged. It's not even a conversation. And then we don't come off as real people, we seem disingenuous."

Remember, it's not about you, it's about the recruit.

"Instead of speaking first to understand a lot of recruiters just speak to be understood. They talk and talk and tell the recruit all sorts of awesome things about their program and the recruit is literally not even listening."

Asking questions and listening will do more to persuade recruits than talking ever will.

"Recruiters make the mistake of thinking they're going to sit down with someone and just woo them with their words. It takes more than that."

Imagine a sales presentation. Telling is not selling! Neither is recruiting.

"Just like a sale, you want to ask as many questions through the process as you can. Do not be the one talking the whole time. No one enjoys a lecture."

Try this as an exercise, the next time you sit down with a recruit, take note of the time before you start. Then throughout the meeting, roughly keep track of the amount of time each of you spend talking. At the end of the meeting, assess if you could have asked more questions and done more listening and what effect that may have had on the meeting.

The Third Sin Of Recruiting
Underestimating the Amount of Work Required to Succeed at Recruiting

The single biggest mistake universally agreed upon by everyone I interviewed was that most recruiters simply underestimate the amount of work it takes to be a great recruiter.

"People never want to be part of the process, but they want to be part of the outcome. Think about how great the recruiting outcome will eventually be—everyone will want to be a part of that, but only some of our people actually will. If you want to be a part of the outcome, you have to grind through the process. That process is recruiting, and its hard work and pure hustle. You have to hustle, hustle, hustle. Remember that great things are not built overnight.

You just have to be consistent and take pride and feel fulfillment in the process. Come up with a good game plan, seek as much advice as you possibly can, find your style of recruiting by talking to others to see what works, and then just go freaking bust it!"

In order to be successful at recruiting, you must be committed to the full process, not just pieces of it.

"Recruiters make the mistake of thinking that recruiting is a process where they just try and sign somebody up, try and get them to come on a sales trip, try and get them to a few trainings. It takes so much more than that. It takes weekly meetings. It takes making phone calls. It takes every action necessary to make these people feel that you genuinely care about them."

Being successful at recruiting has the same requirement as being successful at sales, hard work!

"The biggest mistake recruiters make is they don't work! They feel like recruiting is going to occur by happenstance, that people are just going to come to them. You got to go hustle! You have to be relentless

in your prospecting. Think of selling— if you want to sell accounts and you're getting told no, what are you going to do? Are you going to go home and play Xbox and hope to get accounts? What do you do!? You go knock more doors. Hard work is the great equalizer in recruiting."

You need to be prepared to feel like a rookie again. You need to be willing to be out of your comfort and feel dumb again.

"Aspiring recruiters make the mistake of underestimating the amount of effort it takes to recruit. It takes a lot of work and energy, especially when you're first starting. It's the exact same effort that it took you as a first-year rep to learn how to sell, and for a lot of would-be recruiters they just don't want to make an effort."

"Recruiters underestimate how much work they have to put in to recruit a proper team. Honestly, it's incredible how many people you need to talk to. I don't think most recruiters are prepared for it. My own managers will come to me and say, 'All my guys fell off!' I say let me see your stats real quick. How

many people have you signed this year? They say ten people, but only four have stuck. I say okay cool well your stats are as good as mine. You're just not reaching out to enough people!"

At the end of the day, recruiting has very little, if nothing, to do with natural ability or even developed talent. Hard work is the great equalizer because it gives to the least talented recruiter the same opportunity as it does to the best recruiter. If you are willing to escalate your level of work ethic to never-ending heights, it will be impossible for you to fail as a recruiter.

Conclusion

Thank you for reading *The Seven-Figure Summer: How To Build A Door-To-Door Sales Empire.* You now understand how to drive insane quantities of recruits into your pipeline, how to identify the best ones, how to present your opportunity in a way that gets them stoked, how to lock down any recruit, and how to grow a sales company while avoiding some of the most common pitfalls!

This book should act like a living mentor for you. Return to it often. Apply the techniques thoughtfully, one at a time. Test the ideas found within and read the book over and over again. As you progress as a recruiter, you will see things in this book that you didn't see before. If you skipped over the chapter summary and applications, go back and complete them. You now possess the best recruiting knowledge of the door-to-door industry. But remember that knowledge is not power, applied knowledge is! I hope the information in this book changes the trajectory of your career for the better.

Appendix

Contributing Experts & Thanks

A thank you to the titans of business ideology who's concepts are echoed in this book:

Casey Baugh
Body Gardner
Cody Veibell
Jared Young
Scott Brown
Jason Brown
Grant Cardone
Steven Covey
Dale Carnegie
Jim Rohn
Napoleon Hill
John C. Maxwell

A special thank you to our millionaire recruiters that generously opened their playbooks for the next generation of recruiters to learn from. We are hungry to achieve the same level of success you have.

Also, a call to the world's other top recruiters. Did you earn one million dollars plus last year through recruiting? We all would be deeply grateful to hear your insights on the subject. Please email sixfiguresummer@gmail.com to schedule an interview with the author.

Finally, an extra special thanks to you, the reader. The fact that you are interested enough in your personal development to read this book puts you in the top percentile of professionals in the world. I wish you the best of luck on your journey and would love to hear any feedback you may have. Thank you!

Your 100 List

Look through your phone contacts, social media connections, yearbook, the rosters of any organization you belong to, and anywhere else where you might find the names of people with whom you connections. As you do, think about who of these you would love to work with, that would do well at sales, or that might know someone that would do well at sales (connectors). Write their name and how you know them, for example: "Instagram".

After completing this list, look through it and ask yourself, "who would be my dream recruit" and "who would be easy to recruit." Circle ten of these individuals.

Then make a plan of action for each one. For example: "text to grab lunch" or "start engaging with social media content."

Lastly, take action! Don't wait till you're "more prepared". Just get started now! Success in recruiting is more about starting and not quitting than it is about preparation and knowledge!

	Name	Source	Next Step
1.			
2.			
3.			
4.			
5.			
6.			
7.			
8.			
9.			
10.			
11.			
12.			
13.			
14.			
15.			
16.			
17.			
18.			
19.			
20.			
21.			
22.			
23.			

	Name	Source	Next Step
24.			
25.			
26.			
27.			
28.			
29.			
30.			
31.			
32.			
33.			
34.			
35.			
36.			
37.			
38.			
39.			
40.			
41.			
42.			
43.			
44.			
45.			
46.			

	Name	Source	Next Step
47.			
48.			
49.			
50.			
51.			
52.			
53.			
54.			
55.			
56.			
57.			
58.			
59.			
60.			
61.			
62.			
63.			
64.			
65.			
66.			
67.			
68.			
69.			

Name	Source	Next Step
70.		
71.		
72.		
73.		
74.		
75.		
76.		
77.		
78.		
79.		
80.		
81.		
82.		
83.		
84.		
85.		
86.		
87.		
88.		
89.		
90.		
91.		
92.		

Name	Source	Next Step
93. _____	_____	_____
94. _____	_____	_____
95. _____	_____	_____
96. _____	_____	_____
97. _____	_____	_____
98. _____	_____	_____
99. _____	_____	_____
100 _____	_____	_____

Recommended Reading

- The 10X Rule by Grant Cardone

- The 7 Habits of Highly Effective People by Dr. Stephen R. Covey

    •Habit 2: Begin with the end in mind.
    •Habit 4: Think Win Win
    •Habit 5: Seek first to understand, then to be understood.

- The Speed of Trust by Stephen M. Covey

- How to Win Friends and Influence People by Dale Carnegie

- The 15 Invaluable Laws of Growth by John C. Maxwell

- The 21 Irrefutable Laws of Leadership by John C. Maxwell

- The 7 Habits of Highly Effective People by Dr. Stephen R. Covey

- Leaders Eat Last by Simon Sinek

- Ride of a Lifetime by Bob Iger

Quotes

"The bigger the why, the easier the how." -Jim Rohn

"The greatness of a man is not in how much wealth he acquires, but in his integrity and his ability to affect those around him positively." -Bob Marley

"If you have an instinct to act on a goal, you must physically move within 5 seconds or your brain will kill it. The moment you feel an instinct or a desire to act on a goal or a commitment, do it!" Mel Robbins

"Most people only work enough so that it feels like work, whereas successful people work at a pace that gets such satisfying results that work is a reward. Truly successful people don't even call it work; for them, it's a passion. Why? Because they do enough to win!" -Grant Cardone

"If you wish to influence an individual, tell them a compelling story." -Annette Simmons

"Stories are powerful because they transport us into other people's worlds." -Paul Zak

"A story is a way to say something that can't be said any other way." -Flannery O'Connor

"If you're going to have a story, have a big story, or none at all." -Joseph Campbell

"All human beings have an innate need to hear and tell stories and to have a story to live by." -Harvey Cox

"Stories are the single most powerful weapon in a leader's arsenal." —Howard Gardner, Harvard University

"Many people don't realize the extent to which stories influence our behavior and even shape our culture." -Lawrence Shapiro

"A story can go where facts and analysis is denied admission: our hearts. Facts can persuade people, but it doesn't inspire them to act. To do that, you need to tell a story that fires the imagination and stirs the soul." -Harrison Monarth

"If stories come to you, care for them. And learn to give them away where they are needed. Sometimes a person needs a story more than food to stay alive."
-Barry Lopez

If you help others with all your might
to achieve the goals within their sight
the strength you derive from their delight
will pull you up to greater heights.
-Roy Lee Barrett

"The goal of all leaders should be to work themselves out of a job. When mentored and coached properly, the junior leader can eventually replace the senior leader, allowing the senior leader to move on to the next level of leadership." -Jocko Willink

"Good is the enemy to great." -Jim Collins

"The bigger the why, the easier the how." -Jim Rohn

"The greatness of a man is not in how much wealth he acquires, but in his integrity and his ability to affect those around him positively." -Bob Marley

"The bigger the why, the easier the how."

- Jim Rohn

"If you have an instinct to act on a goal, you must physically move within 5 seconds or your brain will kill it. The moment you feel an instinct or a desire to act on a goal or a commitment, do it!" -Mel Robbins

"Most people only work enough so that it feels like work, whereas successful people work at a pace that gets such satisfying results that work is a reward. Truly successful people don't even call it work; for them, it's a passion. Why? Because they do enough to win!" -Grant Cardone

"If you wish to influence an individual, tell them a compelling story." -Annette Simmons

"Stories are powerful because they transport us into other people's worlds." -Paul Zak

"A story is a way to say something that can't be said any other way." -Flannery O'Connor

"If you're going to have a story, have a big story, or none at all." -Joseph Campbell

"All human beings have an innate need to hear and tell stories and to have a story to live by." -Harvey Cox

"Stories are the single most powerful weapon in a leader's arsenal." -Howard Gardner, Harvard University

"You can have everything in life you want if you will just help enough other people get what they want." -Zig Ziglar

Thoughts, Takeaways & Notes